W9-CMF-158

香祥生福
wacoal

PRIVATE EYES
NYC TAXI

EXTREME Spot the Difference

CITIES OF THE WORLD

40 High-Resolution Photo Puzzles

THUNDER BAY
P·R·E·S·S
San Diego, California

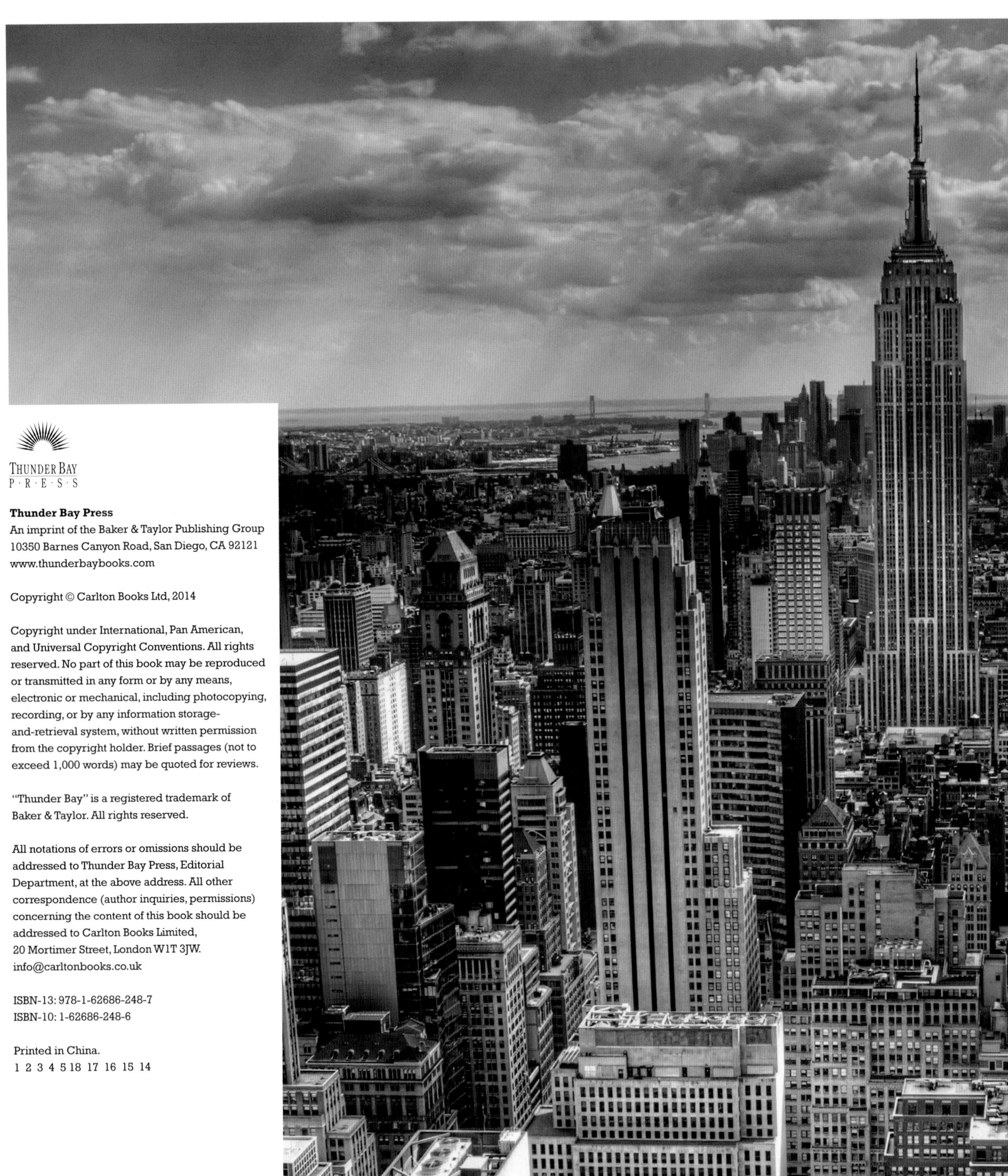

THUNDER BAY
P·R·E·S·S

Thunder Bay Press
An imprint of the Baker & Taylor Publishing Group
10350 Barnes Canyon Road, San Diego, CA 92121
www.thunderbaybooks.com

All notations of errors or omissions should be addressed to Thunder Bay Press, Editorial Department, at the above address. All other correspondence (author inquiries, permissions) concerning the content of this book should be addressed to Carlton Books Limited, 20 Mortimer Street, London W1T 3JW. info@carltonbooks.co.uk

ISBN-13: 978-1-62686-248-7
ISBN-10: 1-62686-248-6

Printed in China.
1 2 3 4 5 18 17 16 15 14

CONTENTS

INTRODUCTION

Scholars past and present are in agreement when it comes to travel: it broadens your mind more than anything else on earth. It makes us "well-rounded people," and isn't that—as civilized human beings in the twenty-first century—what we are all about?

For thousands of years our species has traveled, explored, and adventured this vast sphere we call home. We have scaled the peaks of its highest mountains and trodden down uncharted, dusty paths in areas so remote it takes weeks just to get to them. We have perfected transcontinental travel and have become captains of the seas and masters of the skies. But, perhaps most pertinently, our most fundamentally human achievement has been to lay foundations, to assemble places where we can all live together in peace and harmony. Over the past few centuries, we have constructed ever-more complex and exciting metropolises, tailor-made to suit our evolving commands and desires. Ranging from ancient conurbations to ultramodern cityscapes, the traditional to unconventional, these highly developed and populated regions are not identical collections of architecture. Every single city in the world is different. Unique. Some grow tall, some grow wide. Some are old. Many are new. Every city has its central, familiar components, but—as you'll discover in this book—each city has its own personality, too. From the rolling hills and stretched out highways of L.A. to the majesty of titanic skyscrapers and chaotic marketplaces in Hong Kong to sun-drenched Cape Town's position at sea level on the South Atlantic ocean—cities around the world have *enormous* variety.

It isn't just travel that broadens your mind though. Puzzles do too. Throughout human history, not only has mankind sought to adventure the globe, we have also devised inventive ways of expanding and probing our minds. Mankind's love of puzzles, riddles, and brainteasers dates back thousands of years and as we have evolved, so, too, have the puzzles. This book is the pinnacle of visual challenge. Inside you'll find forty stunning images of the world's most captivating cities. Each one comes with its own set of conundrums and questions. What's missing? What's

changed? What's been added? Have I been here? And, can I go there now, please?

By turning the page, you are instantly transported to many brilliant cities—no doubt hundreds or even thousands of miles away! Armchair traveling has never been so exciting! You can navigate all around the globe without leaving the comfort of your home.

Each city included within is not just a feast for your eyes, but a challenge for your brain. As predominantly visual creatures we make sense of our world with our eyes. It's the main reason why people have come to love Spot the Difference puzzles so much over the years. They naturally complement the way our brains work; the visual stimulus offers our brains—via our ever-wandering eyes—a problem it can't wait to solve.

Humans have been creating puzzles for each other for centuries, though it hasn't been until recent times that we have shared our love of puzzles as entertainment. Combining high-resolution photography with technology capable of making the most minute changes, the book you now hold in your hands represents modern puzzle challenges at their best, as well as a unique perspective of the world's greatest cities. From blink-and-you-miss-them differences to very obvious ones indeed, *Extreme Spot the Diffference: Cities* is guaranteed to entertain and test you in a way you've never experienced before.

But spotting the difference between two images, or solving puzzles in general, is not just about finding the answers. The important part is accepting the challenge to begin with, getting into the zone, and deliberately setting out to complete a set of tasks that exercise your brain power. Interact with what you see on the pages of this book; by doing so you flex and test your brain muscles and, if the task is completed, achieve something significant. Something to feel good about. And that's what's important: completing something that you know won't be easy.

With all that in mind, accept the challenge this unique and refreshing book has to offer. You'll be rewarded not only with a massive sense of achievement, but your brain will also transform into a leaner, quick-thinking super-computer—a puzzle-solving machine. In the process you may even ignite a passion for solving puzzles that you'll take with you in all areas of life.

From the graffiti-covered walls of Berlin to the awe-inspiring landmarks of Rio de Janeiro, stopping off en route at Tripoli or Kyoto, embark on a trip to the world's favorite cities without ever having to leave your chair—it will broaden your mind more than you ever thought possible. So, which city will you travel to first? The challenge is set... off you go!

HOW TO PLAY

There are forty puzzles in *Extreme Spot the Difference: Cities*. Each has their own complex and unique aesthetic just like the city itself. There are fifty differences per city to find. Best to get comfy.

The puzzle changes are an entertaining mix of the obvious (once you have seen them), and the ingenious. As well as being a supreme test of your observation skills, we are confident that you will find this book lots of fun, and it will keep you occupied for hours!

With 2,000 extreme differences to find, you are going to have your work cut out as you attempt to identify all of the changes, so here are a few handy hints and tips to help you on your way.

Before you begin, have a pen and some paper on hand so you can write down the coordinates of the differences as you find them. The original unaltered photograph is shown on the left page, followed by the changed version on the right. Note the pink coordinate on your paper, and then the blue coordinate as this is how you will find them listed on the answer key. The answer key appears immediately after each puzzle.

To help with your hunt, we've included a unique aid for you—the Spotter's Grid. Place it over the picture to isolate a small section, then easily compare with its near twin on the other page. Circling the differences on the Spotter's Grid will also allow you to share the puzzles with others without giving away all the answers. Wipe it clean after each puzzle to use it again and again. Armed with your Spotter's Grid and your powers of observation, all that's left to say is best of luck and happy hunting!

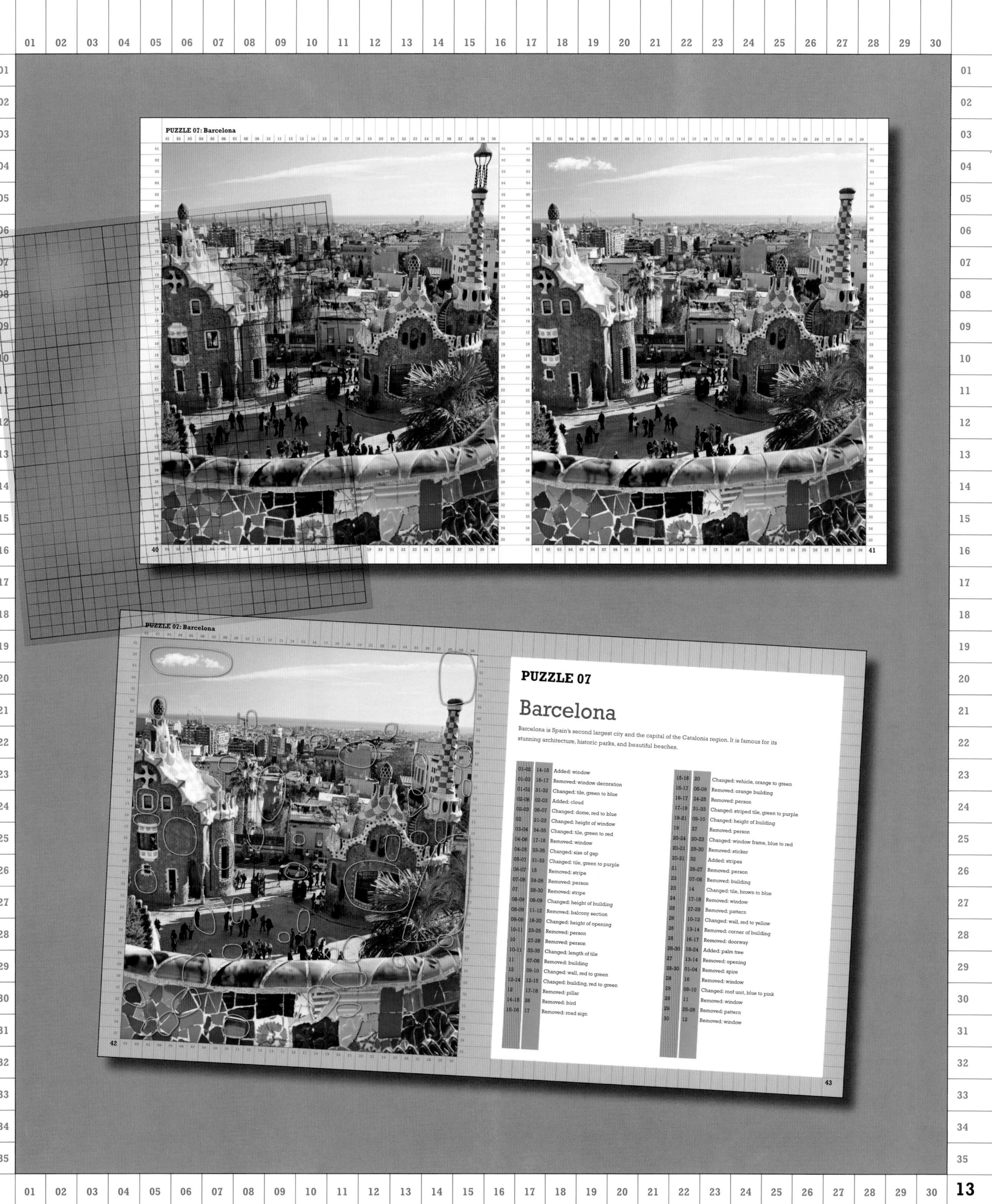

PUZZLE 07: Barcelona

PUZZLE 07

Barcelona

Barcelona is Spain's second largest city and the capital of the Catalonia region. It is famous for its stunning architecture, historic parks, and beautiful beaches.

01-02	14-15	Added: window
01-03	16-17	Removed: window decoration
01-02	31-32	Changed: tile, green to blue
02-08	02-03	Added: cloud
02-03	06-07	Changed: dome, red to blue
02	21-22	Changed: height of window
03-04	34-35	Changed: tile, green to red
04-06	17-18	Removed: window
04-05	33-35	Changed: size of gap
05-07	31-33	Changed: tile, green to purple
06-07	15	Removed: stripe
07-08	24-26	Removed: person
07	28-30	Removed: stripe
08-09	08-09	Changed: height of building
08-09	11-12	Removed: balcony section
08-09	18-20	Changed: height of opening
10-11	23-25	Removed: person
10	27-28	Removed: person
10-11	33-35	Changed: length of tile
11	07-08	Removed: building
12	09-10	Changed: wall, red to green
12-14	12-15	Changed: building, red to green
12	17-18	Removed: pillar
14-15	26	Removed: bird
15-16	17	Removed: road sign
15-16	20	Changed: vehicle, orange to green
16-17	08-09	Removed: orange building
16-17	24-25	Removed: person
17-19	31-33	Changed: striped tile, green to purple
19-21	09-10	Changed: height of building
19	27	Removed: person
20-24	20-23	Changed: window frame, blue to red
20-21	29-30	Removed: sticker
20-21	32	Added: stripes
21	26-27	Removed: person
23	07-08	Removed: building
23	14	Changed: tile, brown to blue
24	17-18	Removed: window
25	27-28	Removed: pattern
26	10-12	Changed: wall, red to yellow
26	13-14	Removed: corner of building
26	16-17	Removed: doorway
26-30	18-24	Added: palm tree
27	13-14	Removed: opening
28-30	01-04	Removed: spire
28	16	Removed: window
29	09-10	Changed: roof unit, blue to pink
29	11	Removed: window
29	25-26	Removed: pattern
30	12	Removed: window

恋占いおみくじ

THE PUZZLES

PUZZLE 01: Sydney

PUZZLE 01: Sydney

PUZZLE 01

Sydney

Sydney is the capital of the Australian state of New South Wales and it is the country's most populous city. Its most famous landmark is the Opera House, located on Sydney Harbour.

01–02	04	Changed: top of tower flipped
01	11	Changed: building, red to blue
01	17	Added: fountain
01–02	20	Added: tree
01–06	33–35	Added: boat
03	17	Removed: arch
04	04	Added: flag
04–05	11	Changed: height of dome
05–07	04–05	Changed: height of building
05–06	10–12	Removed: windows
05–06	19–20	Removed: path
05–06	21	Added: tree
06–07	23–25	Changed: length of pier
09	17	Removed: windows
09–10	19–20	Added: giant koala
10	09	Changed: sign flipped
10	21	Changed: height of building
11–12	15	Changed: shape of building
12–13	10–11	Changed: height of building
12	12	Changed: building, brown to blue
13–16	03–05	Added: cloud
13–14	09	Removed: logo
14–15	07	Added: logo
15–16	13–14	Removed: wall
15–16	15	Removed: roof details

15–16	17–18	Added: tree
16	22–23	Removed: sign
17	08	Removed: support
18–19	06–07	Added: opening
18–20	12–13	Added: ramp
19–20	14	Removed: boat
19	23–24	Removed: shadows
20–22	09–12	Changed: building flipped
20–24	28–29	Added: ridge
20	32	Added: buoy
23–25	08	Removed: roof
23–24	12–13	Changed: height of tower
23	14	Changed: color of sculpture
24–25	08–09	Added: windows
25	08–09	Changed: size of façade
25	31	Removed: pillar
26–30	07	Added: Uluru (Ayers Rock)
26–27	11	Removed: house
26	14–15	Added: building wing
26–30	25–26	Added: section to opera house
28	09–11	Added: building wing
28–30	18–19	Changed: position of boat
29–30	08–09	Removed: bridge tower
29–30	11	Added: boat
30	16	Added: ramp

PUZZLE 02: Florence

PUZZLE 02

Florence

The historic city of Florence is the capital of the Tuscany region in central Italy. It was the cradle of the Renaissance period and its legacy of art, culture, and architecture has made it a popular tourist destination.

01–02	11–12	Added: buildings
01–02	21–23	Added: tower
02	34–35	Added: window
03	24	Removed: window
03–04	18–19	Removed: windows
04–07	16–18	Changed: dome, red to green
04	26	Removed: window
04–05	29	Added: window
04–07	29–30	Changed: roof, red to green
05–06	23–24	Changed: roof, red to green
05	29	Added: satellite dish
05	34–35	Removed: window
06	09	Added: tower
06–07	20–21	Changed: length of building
07–08	13–14	Changed: height of window
07–08	28–30	Changed: size of building
08	09–11	Removed: spire
08–09	17–19	Removed: window
08	22	Changed: pillar
09–20	18	Changed: size of roof
09–10	25	Removed: window
09–10	32–33	Removed: window
10–11	28	Added: extension to building
11	19	Removed: window
13	25–26	Removed: window
13	28	Added: window

14–16	21	Removed: building
14–17	26–27	Changed: roof, red to green
16	19	Removed: window
16–19	33	Changed: size of roof
17	25–26	Removed: window
17	35	Added: window
18	32	Removed: window
19–20	22–23	Removed: window
19	28	Added: window
19–20	32	Changed: size of building
19–20	35	Removed: window
20	29	Removed: window
20	33	Removed: satellite dish
21–23	11–15	Removed: dome support
24	06–07	Added: ball and cross
24–26	15	Added: dome section
24–27	24	Changed: roof, red to green
24–25	26–27	Removed: window
24	34–35	Removed: window
27–30	11–13	Changed: height of hill
27–28	22	Changed length of building
27–30	25–35	Changed: building
28	16–18	Removed: window
29–30	21–22	Added: building
28	16–18	Removed: window
29–30	21–22	Added: building

PUZZLE 03: New York City

PUZZLE 03: New York City

PUZZLE 03

New York City

The most populous urban area of the United States, New York City is one of the most influential cities in the world both culturally and commercially. It features many architectural icons including the Statue of Liberty and the Empire State Building.

01–02	12	Changed: roof, grey to green
01–02	28	Added: cow
01–02	30–31	Added: air conditioner
02–03	25	Removed: panel
02–03	31–32	Changed: height of units
03	32	Changed: seat, red to blue
04–09	07–15	Added: building
05–06	29–30	Changed: height of annex
07–09	16–17	Changed: height of building
08–10	23–24	Added: building level
09	14	Removed: roof unit
10–11	34–35	Changed: unit, yellow to grey
11–12	12–14	Changed: tower colors
11–12	17–23	Added: building
12–15	25–26	Removed: floor
13–14	11–14	Changed: height of building
13–14	28–29	Added: number
13	30	Added: window
13–14	33–34	Changed: height of façade
14–15	31–32	Removed: water tank
15–16	16	Changed: roof, blue to green
15–17	28–30	Changed: height of pyramid
16–17	10–11	Changed: tower, yellow to grey
16–18	10	Added: buildings
16	32	Added: snowman

17–18	09	Added: bridge tower
17	10–12	Changed: height of stripe
17	30–31	Changed: roof unit, blue to red
17–18	31	Changed: rooftop detail
18	23	Removed: window
18–19	33–34	Changed: height of building
19	17–18	Changed: height of building
20–21	11–14	Changed: added windows
20	12–14	Changed: wall
20–21	22–23	Changed: width of building
20–21	28	Removed: window
21–22	17	Removed: pyramid roof
21–22	26–27	Added: roof garden
22–23	29–30	Changed: cover, blue to red
22–24	04–06	Added: King Kong
22–24	23	Changed: size of roof
23	26–27	Changed: height of tower
23–24	28–29	Changed: window
25–27	27	Changed: wall, green to pink
26–27	01	Added: eclipse
26–30	14–24	Added: window reflection
26	31	Changed: container, red to blue
27	30–31	Changed: size of roof
29	29–30	Added: smoke
30	31–32	Added: water tank

PUZZLE 04: Berlin

PUZZLE 04

Berlin

Berlin is Germany's capital located on the River Spree. It is a center of commerce, culture, and science, and home of the famous Brandenburg Gate.

01–04	04–06	Added: cloud
01–04	12–13	Changed: width of building
01	14–16	Removed: statue
01	34–35	Removed: statue
02	19–20	Removed: window
03–04	17	Removed: window
03	31–32	Removed: person
03	34–35	Removed: person
03–04	23–24	Changed: width of steps
04	10	Removed: vase
04	12–14	Removed: column
05	08	Removed: ornament
06–07	04–05	Removed: statue
06–07	07	Changed: circle, yellow to green
06–07	09	Removed: open window
06–07	13–14	Removed: archway statue
06–07	15–16	Removed: statue
06	26–27	Removed: person
07	26–27	Removed: person
08	30–31	Removed: person
09	08–10	Removed: building
09–10	17	Removed: window
11–12	10	Removed: roof section
11–12	19–21	Removed: arch window
13–14	25–26	Removed: sign
14–15	19–20	Removed: top of column
14–15	17–18	Removed: statue
14–16	20–23	Added: tree
15–17	12–13	Changed: size of roof section
15	27–29	Changed: sign, red to green
16–19	10–11	Removed: buildings
18–20	11–12	Changed: roof, red to green
19	19–21	Added: tree
19–21	23–26	Removed: roof tiles
20–22	03–06	Added: seagull
20–22	13–17	Changed: length of building
21–26	32–35	Added: tree
22–23	13	Changed: roof, blue to grey
22–25	13–16	Changed: statue, green to gold
22–23	22–23	Removed: steps
26	13–14	Removed: roof windows
27–29	11–12	Changed: length of building
27	15–17	Changed: length of building
27–29	18–19	Removed: roof vent
28–29	07–09	Changed: height of building
29–30	17–18	Changed: size of roof
28	22–27	Removed: drainpipe
30	22–24	Removed: window
30	27–28	Removed: roof section
30	33–35	Removed: black line

PUZZLE 05: Cairo

PUZZLE 05

Cairo

Egypt's capital is part of the largest metropolitan area in Africa. Known as the "city of a thousand minarets" it is situated on the Nile River, close to the ancient cities of Giza and Memphis.

01–03	06–08	Removed: tree
01–05	15–16	Changed: height of building
01–02	19–21	Added: satellite dish
01–08	31–35	Added: tree
02	11	Removed: window
03–05	28–30	Changed: wall, blue to pink
05–06	20–21	Added: window
06	11–12	Added: balcony
08	13	Added: window
08	15–16	Added: window
09–11	22–24	Changed: walls, yellow to green
10–12	32–33	Changed: width of roof
10–11	03	Removed: tree
11	06	Removed: tree
11	17–18	Removed: window
12	11–12	Removed: window
12–16	26	Changed: wall, yellow to red
13–16	31	Changed: wall, yellow to red
14	12–13	Added: window
14–15	12–13	Removed: window
14–15	34–35	Changed: size of opening
15–16	02–05	Added: tower
15–16	20–21	Removed: doorway
16–17	22–23	Added: satellite dish
17	06	Removed: balcony
17	10–15	Added: chimney
17–18	28–30	Removed: window
18	24–25	Removed: barrel
18–19	26–27	Changed: door, orange to green
18–19	29	Added: umbrella
19	12–13	Removed: window
20–21	02–03	Removed: building
20–22	11–13	Removed: balconies
20–21	22–23	Removed: window
21–23	32–33	Removed: laundry
21–22	33–34	Removed: window
22–23	17–18	Added: satellite dish
22–23	31–32	Added: window
23–24	05–06	Removed: tree
23	20	Removed: window
24	12	Removed: window
24–25	14–15	Added: water tank
24–25	22–23	Added: awning
25–30	04	Changed: height of building
25–28	21	Changed: wall, brown to green
26–28	27–28	Changed: wall, yellow to pink
26–28	31–34	Changed: wall, yellow to pink
27–30	01–02	Changed: height of building
29	11–12	Removed: window
29–30	27–28	Removed: window

PUZZLE 06: London

PUZZLE 06: London

PUZZLE 06

London

London is the capital of England and the United Kingdom. Situated on the River Thames, the city has been a center of culture and commerce for almost two thousand years.

01–02	19–20	Removed: dome from roof
01–02	21–22	Removed: green rooftop
01–02	24–25	Added: roof section
01–03	32–33	Changed: size of chimney
02–03	05–07	Changed: height of building
02–03	09–10	Changed: length of building
03–04	21	Added: window
03–06	22–23	Added: roof section
04–05	11–12	Removed: boat
04–07	12–13	Changed: height of building
04–05	16–17	Changed: height of building
04–07	18–19	Changed: roof, grey to red
05–06	33–34	Added: roof arch
06–07	29–30	Removed: black panel
08–09	05–06	Removed: background
08	31–32	Removed: window
09–10	13–14	Added: section to building
10–11	25–26	Added: roof section
11–14	06–07	Removed: buildings
11–13	13–15	Added: pigeon
11–14	19–21	Changed: size of building
11	34	Removed: window
14–15	09	Added: boat
15–19	09–10	Removed: building
15–17	15–17	Changed: length of building
17–18	18–21	Changed: dome, silver to green
17–18	24–25	Removed: window
19	13–15	Added: windows
20	21–22	Removed: window
20–21	23–25	Changed: dome, green to red
22	05–06	Removed: building
22–24	08	Changed: roof, blue to red
22–23	09–10	Changed: length of building
22	15–16	Added: tower
23–27	02–06	Added: paraglider
23–24	12–14	Changed: length of building
23–24	29–30	Removed: statue
24–28	20–23	Changed: roof, blue to red
24–25	33	Removed: skylight
24–26	20–21	Added: roof section
25–26	12–13	Removed: square from roof
25–26	24	Removed: window arch
25–26	27–28	Added: archway
25–27	31–33	Added: pigeon
26–28	15–16	Changed: building, red to green
27–28	18–19	Removed: window
28–30	11–12	Changed: height of building
29–30	19–20	Changed: size of rooftop
29–30	28	Removed: crossing
30	31–32	Removed: roof section

PUZZLE 07: Barcelona

PUZZLE 07

Barcelona

Barcelona is Spain's second largest city and the capital of the Catalonia region. It is famous for its stunning architecture, historic parks, and beautiful beaches.

01–02	14–15	Added: window
01–03	16–17	Removed: window decoration
01–02	31–32	Changed: tile, green to blue
02–08	02–03	Added: cloud
02–03	06–07	Changed: dome, red to blue
02	21–22	Changed: height of window
03–04	34–35	Changed: tile, green to red
04–06	17–18	Removed: window
04–05	33–35	Changed: size of gap
05–07	31–33	Changed: tile, green to purple
06–07	15	Removed: stripe
07–08	24–26	Removed: person
07	28–30	Removed: stripe
08–09	08–09	Changed: height of building
08–09	11–12	Removed: balcony section
08–09	18–20	Changed: height of opening
10–11	23–25	Removed: person
10	27–28	Removed: person
10–11	33–35	Changed: length of tile
11	07–08	Removed: building
12	09–10	Changed: wall, red to green
12–14	12–15	Changed: building, red to green
12	17–18	Removed: pillar
14–15	26	Removed: bird
15–16	17	Removed: road sign

15–16	20	Changed: vehicle, orange to green
16–17	08–09	Removed: orange building
16–17	24–25	Removed: person
17–19	31–33	Changed: striped tile, green to purple
19–21	09–10	Changed: height of building
19	27	Removed: person
20–24	20–23	Changed: window frame, blue to red
20–21	29–30	Removed: sticker
20–21	32	Added: stripes
21	26–27	Removed: person
23	07–08	Removed: building
23	14	Changed: tile, brown to blue
24	17–18	Removed: window
25	27–28	Removed: pattern
26	10–12	Changed: wall, red to yellow
26	13–14	Removed: corner of building
26	16–17	Removed: doorway
26–30	18–24	Added: palm tree
27	13–14	Removed: opening
28–30	01–04	Removed: spire
28	16	Removed: window
29	09–10	Changed: roof unit, blue to pink
29	11	Removed: window
29	25–26	Removed: pattern
30	12	Removed: window

PUZZLE 08: Kolkata

Mini RT-13A Bus
Mini Bus
আলমপুর
উল্টাডাঙ্গা
TAXI
Raymond
CROWN
Madanji
PRIYA

PUZZLE 08: Kolkata

PUZZLE 08

Kolkata

Kolkata (Calcutta) is the capital of West Bengal, India, and is the country's oldest commercial port. It was an important trading post under British rule and a focal point in the move towards independence in 1947.

01–04	01–03	Changed: height of building
01	17–18	Added: sign
01–03	30–31	Removed: bus logo
01–02	32–34	Removed: picture
02–03	09–10	Added: sign
02–03	13–14	Changed: sign, red to blue
02	18–19	Changed: hijab, pink to blue
02	23	Added: sign
02–06	34–35	Changed: width of roof
04–06	03–04	Removed: rooftop
04	08–09	Removed: window
04–07	16–18	Changed: bus, blue to green
04	18	Removed: bird
04–05	32	Changed: sun graphic
05–06	19–21	Removed: section from bus
08	24	Removed: bucket
09	15–16	Added: motorcycle
09–12	21–24	Changed: taxi, yellow to pink
10–12	18–20	Changed: taxi, yellow to pink
11–14	20–22	Changed: taxi, yellow to pink
11–12	33–34	Added: cable
12–17	02–03	Changed: height of building
12–13	13–14	Changed: roof, blue to pink
13–14	06–07	Changed: height of building
13–14	28–32	Removed: person

14–15	16–17	Removed: window decoration
14	18	Removed: headlight
16–17	06–07	Changed: wall, yellow to blue
16–17	09–10	Added: roof
17–18	11–12	Removed: sign
17	21–22	Changed: bus panel, yellow to red
17–19	32–33	Removed: license plate
19–20	01	Removed: window
19	11–12	Added: sign
19–21	22	Removed: window decoration
19–20	26–27	Changed: bumper, blue to red
19–24	34–35	Changed: vehicle, grey to red
21–24	01–03	Added: area of greenery
23–24	12–14	Added: sign
24–25	09	Removed: sign
24–25	31–32	Removed: windshield wiper
25–27	14–16	Changed: sign, pink to blue
25–26	21–22	Changed: clothing, green to pink
26–29	03–05	Added: paneling
26–27	28	Removed: bus writing
27–28	21	Changed: length of stall
27–28	34	Removed: bus logo
28	07–09	Changed: cloth, yellow to red
29–30	09–11	Removed: sign
29–30	34–35	Removed: headlight

PUZZLE 09: Boston

PUZZLE 09: Boston

PUZZLE 09

Boston

The capital of Massachusetts is one of the United States' oldest cities, shaped by a variety of cultural influences and a rich history. With more than 100 colleges and universities, the Greater Boston area includes the world-famous Harvard University.

01	13–15	Changed: height of building
01–03	33–35	Added: roof section
02–06	14–17	Removed: buildings
02–04	24–25	Removed: building extension
02	27–28	Added: skylights
02–03	31–32	Changed: building opening
03–04	13–14	Added: light
03–06	22–23	Added: lawn
05–06	09–11	Added: building
06–08	13–14	Changed: roof, green to red
06	18–19	Changed: roof, red to green
07–08	09–11	Removed: building
08	22–23	Removed: rooftop opening
09–12	19–20	Changed: size of building
09–11	23–25	Changed: size of building
09–12	27–28	Changed: roof, red to green
09–12	30–31	Added: building side
10	05–06	Removed: roof antenna
10–13	06	Added: windows
12–14	28–30	Changed: size of building
14–16	34–35	Changed: size of building
15–16	07–09	Changed: size of building
15–16	26–28	Changed: size of building
16–18	10–11	Removed: building
16–18	13–14	Changed: size of roof

17–18	34	Removed: vehicle
18–19	12	Changed: size of building
18–19	20–21	Added: ramp
18–21	24	Added: floors
19–21	16–17	Changed: size of building
19–20	26–28	Changed: lights, yellow to red
19–20	30–31	Removed: vehicle and lights
20–21	28–30	Changed: size of building
21–24	17	Added: bridge
21	30–33	Added: background light
22–23	10–11	Removed: building
23	21	Removed: roof lights
23–27	09–10	Removed: island
23–27	32	Removed: roof stripe
23–26	33–35	Changed: size of building
24	21–23	Removed: roof stripe
24–25	27–28	Added: roof section
24–25	29	Added: building lights
25–27	17	Removed: building
26	20–21	Added: building front
26–27	25–26	Added: roof section
26–27	28	Added: building lights
26–27	30–31	Removed: box on roof
26–28	34–35	Changed: size of building
29–30	31–33	Added: floors

PUZZLE 10: Cape Town

PUZZLE 10: Cape Town

PUZZLE 10

Cape Town

Cape Town is South Africa's second most populous city and its legislative capital, as the location of the country's National Parliament.

01–05	04–06	Added: cloud
01	14	Removed: port section
01–03	21	Changed: shape of land
01–04	26–27	Changed: length of jetty
02–03	18–19	Removed: dock
03–04	20–21	Changed: length of building
05–06	16–17	Added: building
05–06	23–24	Removed: jetty
06–07	14	Removed: buildings
06–07	22	Removed: concrete
06–07	26	Added: marina
07–08	20–21	Added: building
07	24–25	Added: marina
08–11	16–17	Changed: size of marina
08–09	20–21	Added: building
08	29	Removed: foam
09–10	13	Changed: length of building
11–13	18–19	Removed: buildings
11–12	26–27	Changed: length of building
11–16	28–29	Removed: cliff edge
12–16	08–09	Changed: shape of mountain
12–14	32–33	Added: rocks and foam
13	27–28	Removed: clearing
14–19	02–03	Added: cloud
15–16	23–24	Added: trees
16–18	17–18	Changed: size of park
17	22–23	Removed: tree
17–18	24–25	Removed: trees
18–21	19–20	Changed: size of opening
18–19	22	Added: tree
18–19	23–24	Added: tree
18–19	27	Removed: plants
19–21	13–15	Changed: shape of hill
21	25–26	Removed: building
22–23	18	Added: lawn
23	23	Removed: sand trap
23–24	33–34	Removed: rocks and foam
24–27	18–19	Changed: field, brown to green
24–25	21–22	Changed: length of building
24–25	25–26	Added: building section
25	28	Removed: tree
25–26	17	Removed: red building
25–30	04–05	Added: cloud
26–30	11–12	Changed: size of hill
27–28	20	Removed: tent
28–29	19–20	Removed: row of trees
29–30	21–22	Removed: building
29	23	Removed: sand trap
30	07–08	Changed: shape of mountain
30	25–26	Changed: building

PUZZLE 11: Melbourne

33
STATION
my metro
CITY CIRCLE TRAM
KEEP LEFT

my metro
CITY CIRCLE TRAM
CITY CIRCLE TRAM
33

PUZZLE 11

Melbourne

Melbourne is the capital of the state of Victoria, Australia, and is the country's second most populous city. It is widely regarded as Australia's cultural capital with a rich tradition of literature, performing arts, and cinema.

01-02	17-18	Added: lamp
01	29	Changed: light, white to green
01	34	Removed: bumper
02	09–10	Changed: flag, blue to red
02–04	13–14	Removed: pillars
02	22–23	Changed: "5" to "3"
02	32	Added: sign
03	13	Removed: arch
04–05	26–28	Changed: window
04–05	29	Removed: motif
05–06	19–21	Removed: decoration
05	24	Changed: box, red to green
06–07	06–07	Changed: panel, weathered
06	10–11	Added: dome
06	32	Changed: sign, green to pink
07	19–22	Changed: picture flipped
07	27–30	Removed: handrail
07–09	31	Added: stripe
08–16	20	Changed: panel, yellow to pink
08–10	24	Changed: bar, green to yellow
10	04	Added: platform
10	21	Added: spotlight
10–11	29	Changed: size of motif
11–12	09	Added: round decoration
12–13	26–28	Removed: mirror

12–13	30	Added: stripes
13–24	03–06	Added: cloud
13	25–16	Removed: clock
13–14	28	Removed: rail
15–18	29–30	Changed: vehicle, red to blue
15–20	33–34	Removed: street markings
17	26	Changed: writing flipped
17	30	Changed: direction of arrow
18–19	18–20	Changed: wall, red to yellow
19	29–31	Added: person
20	13	Added: decoration
20–21	14–15	Removed: light
22	17	Removed: decoration
23–24	27	Removed: sign
25	14	Added: person
25	14–15	Removed: hook
26–30	13–14	Removed: wire
26–27	22–24	Changed: wall, red to green
26–30	33–35	Added: kangaroo
27	29–30	Changed: height of person
28–29	16–17	Changed: clock rotated
28	28	Changed: traffic light, red to green
28–30	34	Removed: road stripe
29	08	Added: flag
29–30	29–32	Changed: direction of person

PUZZLE 12: Marseille

PUZZLE 12: Marseille

PUZZLE 12

Marseille

France's second largest city is situated on the Mediterranean coast in an area that has been inhabited for almost 30,000 years. Its climate, culture, and history make it a popular holiday resort.

01–02	06–07	Changed: height of building
01–02	11–12	Changed: length of building
01–02	12–15	Changed: depth of second story
01–03	19–20	Changed: fence, red to green
01–02	21–22	Removed: tire
01–02	32–33	Removed: window
02–07	01–03	Changed: height of building
02	09–10	Removed: window
03–05	07	Removed: top story of building
03	16	Removed: sign
03	16–17	Removed: person
04–05	23–24	Added: seagull
05–06	12–13	Changed: height of building
06–08	13–15	Changed: windows
07–09	25–26	Removed: reflection
08	06	Added: seagull
09–10	32–34	Added: seagull
11–13	09	Changed: extended greenery
11–12	14	Removed: vehicle
13–16	07–08	Changed: height of building
13–14	12–13	Added: window
14–15	16	Changed: cover, blue to red
15–16	06–07	Removed: building
15–16	09–10	Changed: height of building
15–16	15	Added: boat

17–18	07	Changed: height of building
18–19	02–03	Added: seagull
19–21	05–06	Removed: building
19–20	08	Changed: height of building
20–21	08	Changed: building, red to green
22–23	10–12	Changed: building, yellow to green
22–23	13–16	Added: box on pole
22–23	17–19	Added: boat
22–24	30–31	Removed: reflection
23–25	06–08	Changed: building, orange to red
24–27	11–12	Changed: roof, red to green
25	12–13	Removed: window
25–27	17–18	Changed: cover, red to green
26–27	09	Changed: roof, red to green
26–29	19–20	Changed: boat, red to blue
27–28	03–04	Removed: balcony
27–28	05–07	Changed: width of building
28–30	14–16	Changed: building, yellow to green
28–29	21	Added: seat
28–29	22–23	Removed: motor
28–29	25	Removed: stone
29–20	01–03	Removed: tower
29–30	10	Removed: window
30	17–18	Removed: people
30	26–27	Removed: rail

PUZZLE 13: Fez

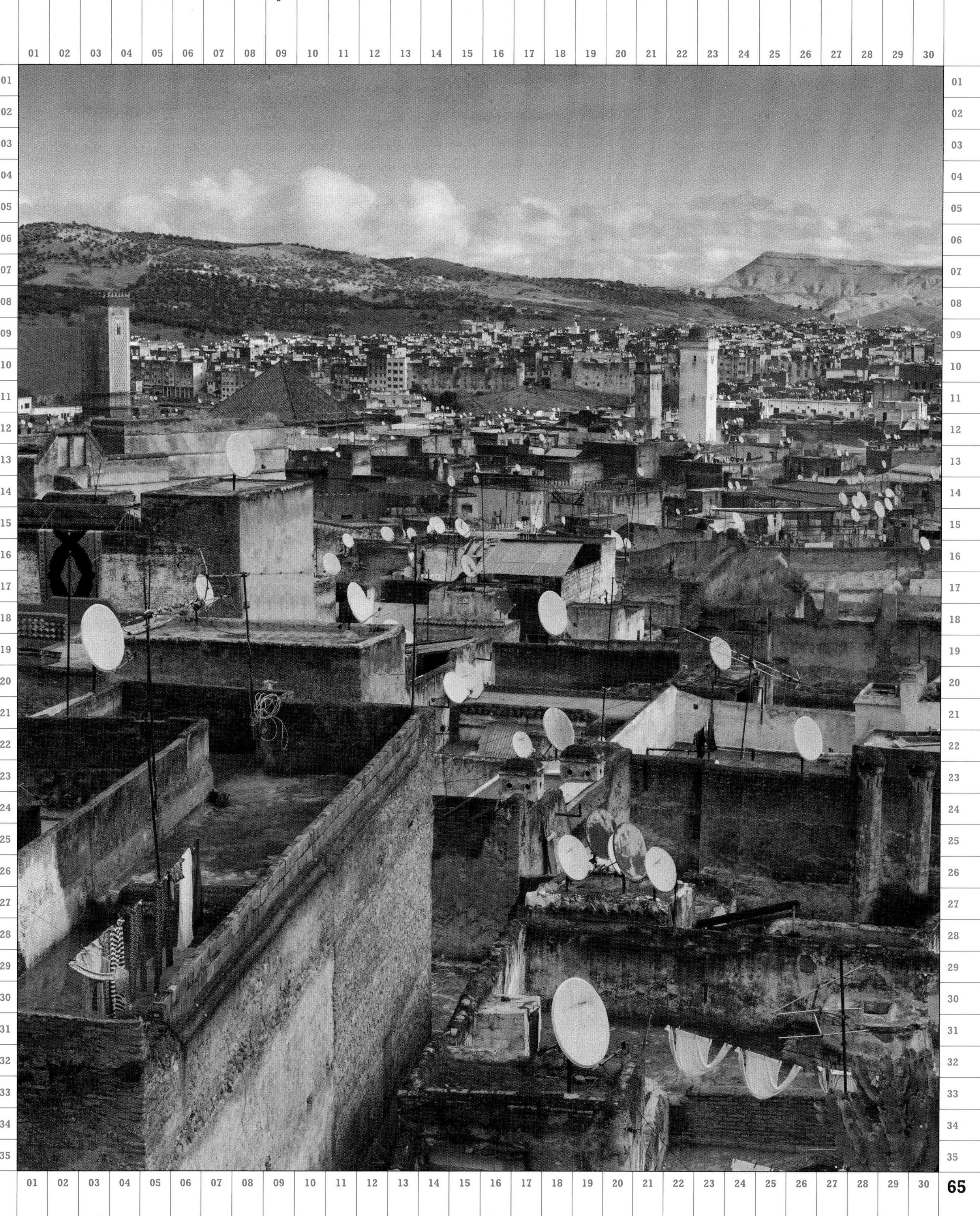

PUZZLE 13: Fez

PUZZLE 13

Fez

Fez is the third largest city of Morocco, famous for its old medinas—labyrinthine market districts. Founded in 859AD, it has been described as the "Mecca of the West."

01–02	10–11	Removed: buildings
01–03	15–17	Changed: rug, brown to green
01–02	18–19	Added: roof tiles
01	22–23	Added: wall
01–02	25–29	Changed: wall, white to green
01–02	30	Removed: post
02–05	31–32	Removed: bricks
03–04	06–07	Removed: top of tower
03–05	12–13	Changed: size of wall
03–04	13–14	Removed: satellite dish
03–04	18–20	Added: satellite dish
04–05	27–30	Added: laundry
06–11	08–09	Added: trees
06–13	22–31	Removed: row of bricks
07–11	10–12	Changed: roof, green to purple
07–08	12–13	Added: satellite dish
08–09	15–16	Removed: antenna
08–10	17–18	Removed: satellite dish
08	22–26	Removed: pole
08–09	31–34	Removed: window
10–11	15	Removed: satellite dish
11–12	19–21	Removed: bar
14–15	08–09	Removed: building
14–16	25–28	Removed: markings on wall
15–17	10–11	Changed: buildings
15–16	17–18	Removed: satellite dish
17–19	15–16	Changed: roof, red to blue
17–18	17–18	Added: satellite dish
18–19	22–23	Added: stone block
19–21	28–30	Removed: satellite dish
20	18–19	Removed: doorway
20–24	28	Changed: wall repaired
21	16	Removed: satellite dish
21–22	19–20	Removed: satellite dish
21	21–22	Removed: laundry
21–22	25–27	Added: satellite dish
22–23	09–11	Changed: height of tower
22–24	23–26	Changed: size of wall
23–27	07–08	Changed: size of mountain
24–26	11–12	Changed: length of building
24–28	14	Changed: roof, grey to red
24–25	16–17	Removed: satellite dish
24–26	32–33	Added: laundry
25–26	15	Removed: satellite dishes
25–26	26–27	Removed: rug
26–27	21–22	Added: satellite dish
27	17–18	Added: wall section
27–30	32–35	Added: plant
29	21	Removed: doorway
30	22–27	Added: wall column

PUZZLE 14: Hong Kong

永興隆窗簾布藝
祥莊香祥生福
馬馬維邦

PUZZLE 14: Hong Kong

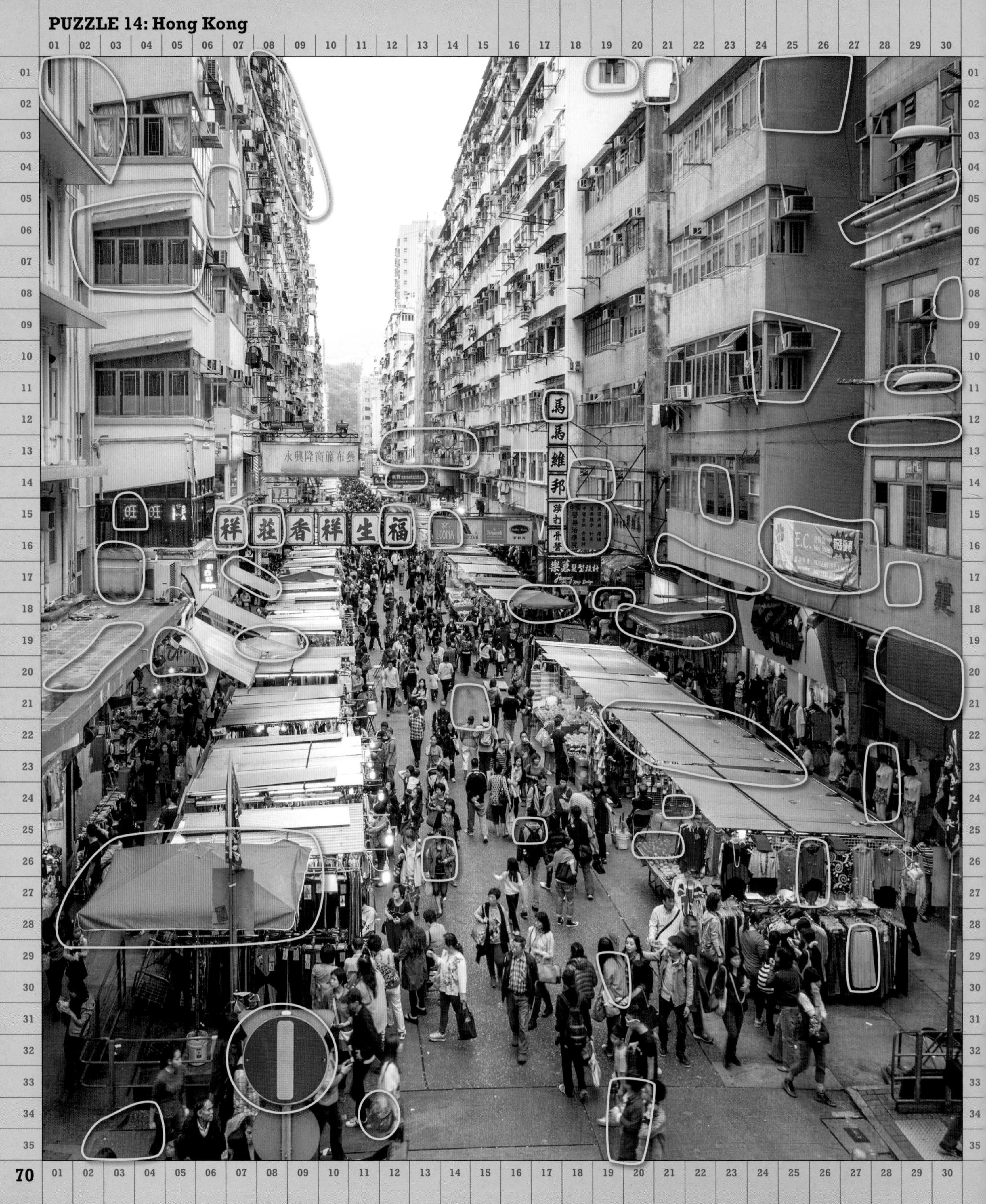

PUZZLE 14

Hong Kong

Hong Kong is a city-state of the People's Republic of China. It belonged to the British Empire from 1842 until 1997, when China resumed sovereignty over the region.

01–03	01–04	Removed: railings
01–04	19–20	Removed: puddles
02–05	05–08	Changed: window
02–09	25–28	Changed: awning, blue to pink
02–04	34–35	Removed: handcart
03–04	15	Added: sign
03–04	16–18	Removed: air conditioner
04–05	19–20	Changed: sign, yellow to pink
06–07	04–06	Removed: window
06–07	15–16	Added: banner
07–08	17	Added: awning
07–09	19	Changed: awning, pink to green
07–10	31–34	Changed: sign rotated
08–09	01–05	Changed: size of building
08	15–16	Changed: writing, red to green
11–12	34–35	Changed: bag, yellow to red
12–14	13	Removed: sign
12–13	14	Changed: sign, green to pink
12	15–16	Changed: writing, red to blue
13–14	15–16	Changed: sign, green to yellow
13–14	26	Changed: jacket, blue to pink
14–15	21–22	Removed: person
16–18	18	Changed: awning, pink to green
16–17	25	Changed: backpack, blue to pink
17–18	11–12	Added: sign
18–19	14	Removed: sign
18–19	15–16	Changed: sign, yellow to blue
19–20	01	Changed: size of window
19–20	18	Removed: sign
19–25	21–23	Added: cover
19–20	29–30	Changed: jacket, red to orange
19–20	33–35	Changed: jacket, red to blue
20–21	01–02	Removed: greenery
20–23	18–19	Changed: covering
20–21	25–26	Changed: fruit, orange to green
21–24	16–17	Removed: pipes
21–22	24	Removed: lamp
22–23	14–15	Changed: window
24–26	01–02	Removed: window
24–26	09–11	Added: window
24–27	15–17	Changed: sign, green to orange
25–26	27	Changed: dress, red to blue
27–30	05–06	Added: pipe
27–30	12–13	Removed: pipe
27	28–30	Changed: skirt, pink to green
28–30	11	Added: lamp
28–29	17–18	Removed: writing on wall
28–30	19–21	Changed: height of board
28	23–25	Added: mannequin
30	08–09	Removed: vent

PUZZLE 15: Madrid

PUZZLE 15: Madrid

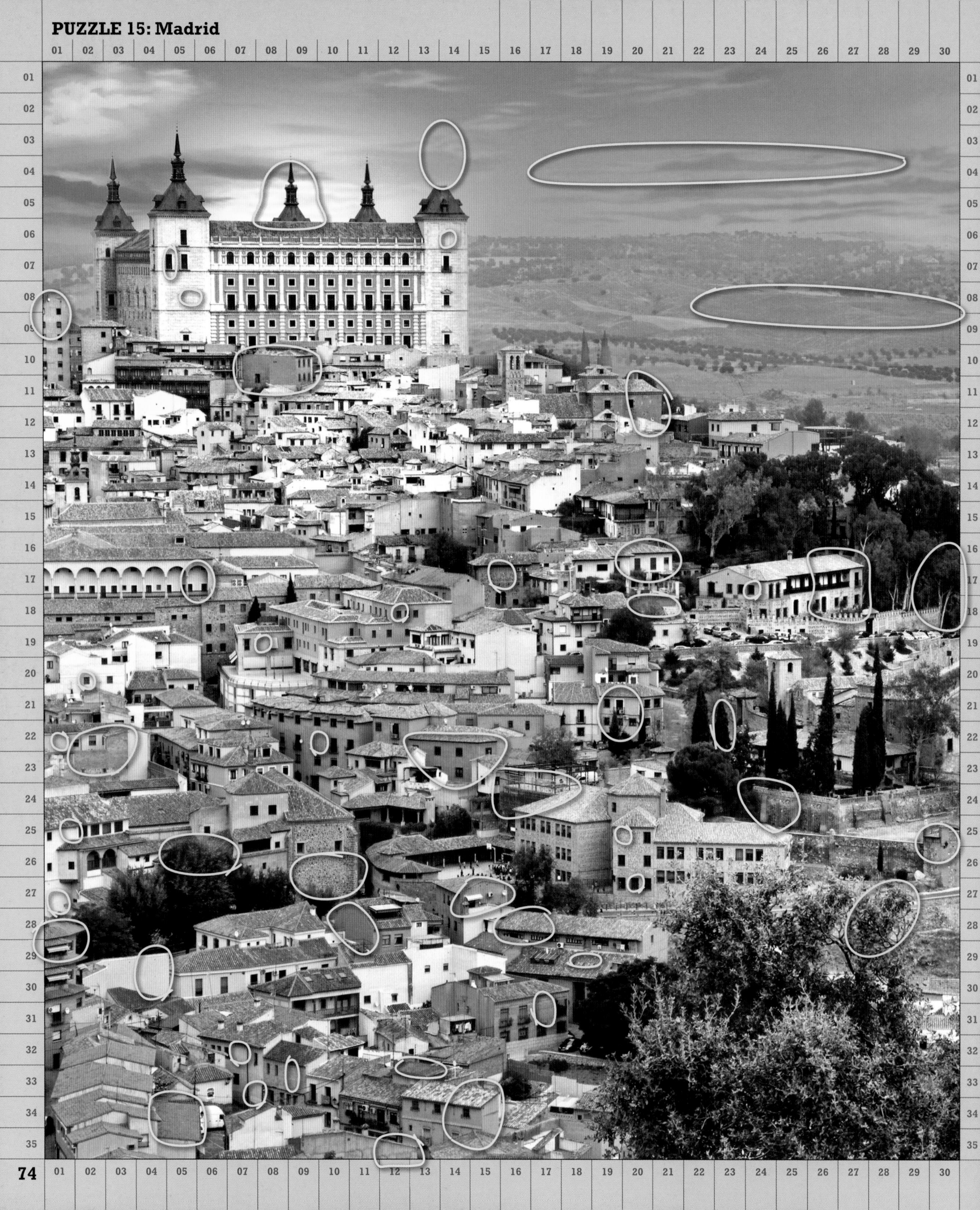

PUZZLE 15

Madrid

Spain's capital is located on the Manzanares River in the center of the country. The area has been occupied since prehistoric times, and has grown into the cultural and financial hub of Southern Europe.

01	08–09	Changed: height of building
01	22	Removed: window
01–02	25	Removed: window
01	27–28	Removed: window
01–02	28–29	Changed: height of building
02	20	Added: window
02–03	22–23	Changed: wall, brown to green
04–07	25–26	Changed: height of tree
04	29–30	Changed: length of building
04–05	34–35	Changed: roof, red to green
05	07	Added: window
05	08	Removed: window
05–06	17–18	Added: archway
07–09	10–11	Changed: building, red to green
07	32	Removed: window
07–08	33–34	Removed: door
08–09	04–06	Added: spire
08	19	Removed: window
09–10	22–23	Removed: window
09–11	26–27	Changed: height of tree
09	33	Removed: window
10–11	27–29	Changed: wall, red to pink
12	18	Added: window
12–13	32–33	Changed: roof, red to green
12–13	35	Changed: width of building
13–14	03–04	Removed: top of spire
13–15	22–23	Changed: building, red to green
14	06	Removed: window
14–16	27	Changed: wall, yellow to pink
14–15	33–35	Changed: width of building
15–16	17	Removed: window
16–18	23–24	Changed: scaffold, green to red
16–17	28	Changed: width of building
17–27	03–04	Added: cloud
17	31	Removed: window
18–19	29	Removed: skylight
19–20	21–22	Changed: wall, red to green
19–20	25	Removed: window
20–21	11–12	Changed: length of building
20–21	16–17	Changed: length of building
20–21	18	Changed: wall, red to green
20	27	Added: window
22–30	08–09	Changed: field
23	21–22	Added: tree
24	17	Added: window
24–25	24–25	Removed: tree
26–27	16–18	Changed: length of building
27–29	27–29	Added: foliage
29–30	16–18	Added: tree
29–30	25–26	Changed: height of building

PUZZLE 16: Rio de Janeiro

PUZZLE 16: Rio de Janeiro

PUZZLE 16

Rio de Janeiro

Rio is Brazil's second largest city. Since its foundation by the Portuguese in 1556, it has grown into one of the world's most popular tourist destinations, famous for its beaches, carnivals, and the iconic statue of Cristo Redentor.

01–02	13	Removed: buildings
01–02	16	Removed: whitecap from water
01–02	19–20	Removed: building
01–02	30–31	Removed: building
02–04	10–11	Changed: height of mountain
02–06	12–14	Changed: shape of mountain
02	22	Removed: tower
02–05	35	Removed: building
03–04	19–20	Changed: height of building
04–08	02–04	Added: cloud
04–05	22–23	Changed: height of building
05–07	4–10	Added: parrot
06	22–23	Changed: height of building
07–09	14–15	Removed: building
07–08	21–22	Changed: size of building
07–08	27–28	Removed: spire
08–09	29–30	Changed: width of building
09–10	21	Changed: height of building
09–10	26–27	Removed: tree
10–11	13–14	Removed: beach
11–14	10–11	Removed: mountain
12–15	26–27	Changed: height of building
13–14	16–17	Removed: buildings
13–19	20–22	Removed: boat and wake
13–15	29–30	Changed: width of building
14	32–34	Added: building
16–17	11	Changed: size of mountaintop
16–17	12–13	Added: woodland
16–18	30–32	Changed: width of building
18–19	16	Removed: buildings
18–19	32–33	Changed: width of building
19–21	12	Removed: buildings
19–20	27–30	Changed: width of building
20–22	12–13	Changed: size of hill
20–24	14–16	Changed: height of woodland
20	24	Removed: boat
21	21–22	Removed: boat
21	23	Removed: boat
21–23	27–28	Changed: height of building
21–23	31–32	Added: building
23–24	17–18	Removed: building
25–26	13	Removed: cave
25–27	28–30	Changed: height of building
26	22	Removed: boat
26	33–34	Changed: width of building
26–27	9–10	Added: King Kong
28–30	11–14	Changed: size of mountain
28–30	26–28	Changed: height of building
28–30	34–35	Added: bush
29–30	32–33	Changed: buildings merged

PUZZLE 17: Prague

01 02 03 04 05 06 07 08 09 10 11 12 13 14 15 16 17 18 19 20 21 22 23 24 25 26 27 28 29 30
01 02 03 04 05 06 07 08 09 10 11 12 13 14 15 16 17 18 19 20 21 22 23 24 25 26 27 28 29 30 31 32 33 34 35

PUZZLE 17: Prague

PUZZLE 17

Prague

The thousand-year-old city of Prague is the capital of the Czech Republic, located on the Vltava River in the northwest portion of the country. It is home to the world's largest ancient castle and its historic center is a UNESCO World Heritage site.

01–04	16–17	Changed: height of second story
01–03	19–20	Changed: roof, red to grey
02–03	02	Added: roof
02–03	08–09	Added: roof section
02–03	32	Added: roof section
04–07	02–03	Changed: roof, red to green
04–06	23–25	Changed: roof, red to grey
04–07	30–32	Changed: wall, yellow to blue
06–08	05–06	Changed: size of roof
06	29	Removed: solar panel
06–07	33	Removed: roof section
08	28	Removed: chimney
09–10	02–03	Added: roof section
09–10	08	Removed: solar panels
09–11	11–14	Changed: roof, red to green
09–10	19–21	Changed: size of building
09–10	28–31	Changed: size of building
10–11	23–24	Added: paving
11–13	04–06	Changed: roof, red to green
11	31–34	Removed: line on roof
13–16	22–24	Changed: pool, brown to green
14–15	25–26	Added: roof section
15–16	28–30	Changed: roof, red to grey
16	27	Removed: roof section
17–19	09–10	Changed: size of building

18–19	13–16	Changed: building, blue to green
18–20	19–20	Removed: shadow
19–20	01–02	Changed: tower, blue to red
19–20	27–28	Removed: vehicles
20	23–24	Removed: horse and cart
21–22	09–10	Removed: roof windows
22–23	01	Changed: roof
22–23	27	Removed: spire
23–25	16–19	Changed: shape of building
23–24	21–23	Added: trees
24–26	06–07	Changed: roof, red to green
24	34–35	Changed: shape of building
25	14–15	Added: awning
26–27	21–23	Added: trees
26–28	24–26	Changed: tower, blue to bronze
26–27	34–35	Removed: sunlight on roof
27–29	01–02	Changed: length of building
27–30	22–24	Changed: roof, brown to green
27–30	29–30	Changed: roof, red to green
28–30	07–09	Changed: size of building
28–30	12–15	Changed: size of building
28–29	17	Removed: roof windows
28–29	32–34	Changed: shape of building
29–30	16–18	Changed: roof, red to green
29–30	33–34	Changed: roof, red to green

PUZZLE 18: Seoul

PUZZLE 18: Seoul

PUZZLE 18

Seoul

Seoul is the capital of South Korea and forms part of the world's second largest metropolitan area. It is situated on the Han River in the northwest of the country. Today it is a major center of technology and commerce.

03	18	Removed: light
03	19	Added: window
03–06	21–22	Added: smoke
04–10	02–08	Added: laser beam
04	23	Changed: water tank, blue to grey
04–05	31–32	Changed: light, yellow to blue
05	12–13	Changed: wall, white to yellow
05	22–23	Added: windows
05	24	Removed: building
05	25	Removed: window
06	14	Added: helicopter
06	15	Changed: light in window
06–07	26	Changed: height of building
07	20–21	Added: frame tower
07	28	Removed: window
07	29	Changed: window, black to red
07	33	Added: motorcycle
07	23	Changed: roof unit, orange to red
08–10	13	Changed: height of building
08–09	24	Changed: wall, red to blue
08	27–28	Changed: height of tower
08	34	Changed: length of hole in bridge
09–10	11–12	Added: buildings
10	25	Added: roof annex
11	26	Added: windows
12	02–09	Added: laser beam
12	25	Changed: wall, red to black
12–13	29	Changed: light, red to green
13–14	25	Added: satellite dish
16–17	30–31	Added: red leaves
17–18	16	Changed: light in window
17–18	29	Changed: sign, green to red
18	19	Removed: roof unit
20	15–16	Removed: building section
21–22	02	Added: flying saucer
21	12	Removed: lights
21	15	Changed: extended window
21–22	20–21	Changed: height of building
22	06–07	Removed: tower
22	17	Removed: light
22–23	18	Changed: width of floor
23	13–15	Added: windows
24	13	Changed: size of light
25–26	33	Changed: light, yellow to red
27–28	01–03	Changed: height of tower
27–28	04	Changed: platform reversed
27–30	12–14	Changed: height of building
29	04	Changed: light, red to blue
29	06	Added: satellite dish
29–30	29–30	Added: light

PUZZLE 19: Edinburgh

PUZZLE 19: Edinburgh

PUZZLE 19

Edinburgh

Scotland's capital is dominated by the Castle Rock, atop which sits Edinburgh Castle, Scotland's most popular tourist attraction.

01–02	23	Removed: window
02	05–10	Changed: width of building
03–05	18	Changed: building, yellow to red
03–04	29–30	Added: windows
04	20	Removed: grey box
05–06	04–05	Removed: chimney
06–09	28–33	Changed: width of building
08–12	08–09	Changed: height of cliff
09–10	04–05	Added: turret
09–10	16	Removed: chimney
09	23	Changed: window unlit
10–11	26–32	Changed: width of building
11	17–18	Changed: width of window
12–14	34–35	Changed: height of building
13	30	Added: window
14–16	15–16	Removed: rocks
15–16	03–05	Removed: castle top
15–19	09–11	Removed: wall markings
15–16	18	Removed: window
16–19	13	Added: grass embankment
16–17	22–23	Changed: window, blue to pink
16–19	25–26	Removed: chimney
16–17	30–35	Changed: crane, blue to red
18–19	16–17	Removed: tower
18–19	30	Changed: windows lit

19–21	14–18	Changed: width of building
19	34–35	Removed: window
20–22	08–10	Changed: length of crane
20	23–25	Added: spire
21–22	26	Added: window
21	27	Removed: window
21	29	Removed: window
21–22	31–32	Removed: window
23–25	06–07	Removed: rooftop
23–26	10–11	Changed: height of wall
23	30–31	Removed: window
24–26	02–04	Added: pigeon
24–25	19	Removed: chimney
25–26	12	Removed: group of people
25–26	25–26	Changed: roof, grey to red
26	21–23	Added: black stripe
26	27–28	Removed: window
26	30	Removed: window
27–28	13–15	Added: building
27–29	31–32	Added: roof extension
28–30	08–09	Added: trees
28	33	Removed: windows
29–30	23–24	Added: wall
29–30	28	Removed: conservatory
29	30	Removed: window

PUZZLE 20: Seville

PUZZLE 20: Seville

PUZZLE 20

Seville

Seville is the capital of Andalusia in southern Spain. It contains the country's only river port and the oldest functioning royal palace in Europe, the Alcázar of Seville.

01–11	01–03	Added: cloud
01–04	11	Removed: buildings
01–03	13	Added: roof
01	22–16	Changed: height of statue
01–04	34–35	Added: tree
02–03	31–32	Added: shadow
02–04	33–34	Removed: people and shadow
03–05	19–20	Changed: roof, orange to green
05–07	14–15	Changed: roof, brown to red
05–06	19–20	Changed: size of building
05–06	32–33	Removed: shadow
06–07	24–25	Removed: tree
06–07	28–29	Added: pigeon
07–08	18–19	Added: top of tower
08–09	16	Removed: windows
09	13	Removed: pole
09–11	18–20	Changed: height of tower
09–10	26–27	Removed: pillar
10–13	31–32	Removed: shadow
11–12	10–11	Removed: building
11–16	16–17	Changed: roof, red to green
11	24–26	Removed: pillar
13–15	14–15	Added: towers
13	18	Removed: window
13–15	19–22	Added: tree
13–15	27–29	Added: dome
14–17	09	Removed: bridge
14	24–25	Added: lamppost
14–16	33–35	Added: pigeon
15–17	22	Removed: vehicle
15	24	Removed: people
16	19	Removed: window
17–18	07	Removed: bridge
18–19	12–13	Changed: size of roof
18	18–19	Removed: window
19–22	02–06	Added: hot air balloon
19–20	15–17	Removed: pillar
20	12	Added: heart
20–21	24–26	Removed: pillar
21–22	15–16	Changed: length of building
21–22	16–17	Removed: dormer
24–25	10–11	Removed: building section
25–26	07–08	Changed: height of building
25–28	12–13	Changed: height of wall
25–29	17–19	Changed: height of wall
25–26	19–20	Changed: dome, blue to red
27–28	16	Changed: length of roof
27–28	34–35	Changed: shape of shadow
30	11–13	Added: foliage
30	14–15	Changed: wall, pink to green

PUZZLE 21: NYC: Times Square

BARCLAYS
RuPaul's
DRAG RACE
NEW SEASON
city outdoor
"THE CROWD GOES WILD!"
—The New York Times
JERSEY BOY
August Wilson Theatre, 245 West 52nd Street
WINNER!
KELSEY GRAMMER
LA CAGE AUX FOLLES
SO MUCH HAPPENED BEFORE DOROTHY DROPPED IN.
WICKED
THE UNTOLD STORY OF THE WITCHES OF OZ
Tonight belongs to...
HANTOM
FRS
DON'T LET THE BED BUGS BITE!
PROTECT-A-BED
GIFTS
TAD'S STEAKS
sbarro
MAMMA MIA!
W 47 St
PRIVATE EYES
NYC TAXI

BARCLAYS
RuPaul's DRAG RACE
NEW SEASON
"THE CROWD GOES WILD!"
JERSEY BOYS
August Wilson Theatre, 245 West 52nd Street
SO MUCH HAPPENED BEFORE DOROTHY DROPPED IN.
WICKED
WINNER! BEST MUSICAL REVIVAL
LA CAGE AUX FOLLES
KELSEY GRAMMER
Tonight belongs to...
PHANTOM
FRS
DON'T LET THE BED BUGS BITE!
PROTECT-A-BED
GIFTS
ELECTRONICS
TADS STEAKS
sbarro
PRIVATE EYES
NYC TAXI

PUZZLE 21

NYC: Times Square

Times Square is an intersection located in Midtown Manhattan, New York City. It is a major commercial and cultural center and its brightly lit Broadway billboards have become iconic around the world.

01–06	13–15	Changed: height of building
01	25	Removed: window
01–02	30–31	Changed: sign, green to orange
02–04	07–11	Changed: width of sign
02	19	Changed: window lit
03	26–27	Added: traffic light
03	33–34	Added: bus headlight
04	03	Removed: logo
04–05	12	Removed: writing
04–06	18–21	Changed: sign
04–07	31–33	Changed: vehicle, red to blue
05–06	10	Changed: windows lit
05–08	25	Changed: sign, blue to red
06–08	12–13	Added: windows lit
06–08	35	Changed: road marking
08	29–30	Removed: pillar
08–13	31–33	Changed: taxi, yellow to pink
09–10	13–14	Added: lamp
09–10	15–17	Changed: height of building
09–11	22–25	Changed: size of poster
09–10	27	Removed: "GIFTS"
09–10	35	Removed: manhole
10–15	01–06	Changed: height of building
11	11	Removed: window
11–12	35	Removed: road markings
13–18	18–23	Changed: sign, green to yellow
13–16	25	Removed: writing
13–14	28	Removed: writing
13	30–31	Added: pillar
14	32	Removed: manhole
14–17	34–35	Removed: road markings
15–16	07–09	Added: decoration
16–19	10–11	Changed: writing, red to green
17–18	30–31	Removed: trash can
18–19	27–28	Removed: text
19	15–16	Removed: "S"
19	31–32	Removed: person
20–21	01–02	Changed: writing, pink to blue
20	06–07	Removed: window
20–25	16–17	Changed: sign, blue to red
20–23	26–27	Changed: width of board
21–22	23–24	Removed: "P"
22–25	03–04	Removed: writing
22–23	15	Removed: writing
22–25	28	Changed: stripe, red to green
24–25	20–21	Removed: eye in mask
27–29	01–02	Removed: lights
27–29	03	Added: lights
28–30	10	Removed: lights
29–30	12–24	Changed: length of building

PUZZLE 22: Siena

PUZZLE 22: Siena

PUZZLE 22

Siena

Siena is a historic city in Tuscany, Italy. It is one of the country's most popular tourist attractions, famed for its museums, art, and architecture, and its local cuisine.

01	15	Added: window
01–05	21–22	Changed: wall, yellow to red
01	29–30	Removed: window
02–03	14–15	Changed: length of building
02	17	Changed: shape of shadow
04–05	29	Added: flowers
05–06	16–17	Added: window
05–07	19–22	Changed: wall, yellow to green
05–06	25–26	Removed: vehicle
06	28–29	Removed: shadow
07	04–06	Added: cloud
07–08	19–20	Removed: window
07–09	28–30	Changed: wall, yellow to pink
08–10	21–22	Changed: height of building
09–12	17–18	Changed: height of building
10	25	Removed: window
10–11	29–30	Removed: vehicle
11	22	Removed: drainpipe
11–12	32–34	Removed: chimney
12	13	Removed: window
12–14	16	Changed: height of building
13	25–26	Added: window
13	29–30	Removed: window
13–15	13	Removed: building
13–14	31–32	Removed: vehicle

14–15	15	Added: window
14–15	33–34	Added: seagull
15	21–23	Added: foliage
15	26	Changed: shutters, green to red
15	27–28	Added: window
15–16	31–32	Removed: doorway
16–17	27	Changed: length of awning
17	10–11	Removed: window
17–19	15–16	Changed: length of building
17	24–25	Removed: chimney
17–22	32–34	Changed: roof, brown to green
18–23	19–24	Removed: ruined building
18	34	Removed: chimney
19–20	14	Changed: colors of laundry
21–22	10	Removed: wall section
23–27	08–09	Changed: dome, blue to red
26	06–07	Removed: window
26	11–12	Added: window
26–29	32–34	Added: bushes
27	04–05	Removed: spire
27–28	14–17	Changed: size of building
28	10	Removed: arch window
30	13	Changed: window, green to red
30	14	Removed: window
30	17–18	Removed: door

PUZZLE 23: Havana

PUZZLE 23

Havana

Cuba's capital, Havana, is a major Caribbean port. Founded by the Spanish conquistador Diego Velázquez de Cuéllar in 1515, the city boasts some of the most diverse architecture in the world.

01–09	19–21	Changed: edge of roof
01	22–24	Added: shutters
01–08	23–25	Changed: balcony, blue to red
01–02	29–30	Added: seated person
04	08	Added: container
04	12–13	Changed: window, blue to red
04–05	27–28	Added: person
04	28–30	Changed: direction of person
05–06	25	Removed: black window
06–07	05–07	Added: tree
07–08	04–05	Added: crane
07	13	Changed: container, blue to green
07	21	Added: lamp
08	24–25	Removed: lamp
08	27–29	Added: sign
09–10	28	Removed: manhole cover
09–13	10	Added: clothesline
10–11	26–28	Changed: people reversed
10–11	34	Removed: square
11	11–12	Removed: window
12–13	02–03	Changed: height of tower
12	11–13	Changed: size of window
12–14	25	Changed: size of sign
13	18	Added: window
13–14	21–22	Removed: balcony
13–28	23–26	Changed: edge of balcony, white to green
14	33	Added: penguin
16–17	29–30	Changed: shirt, red to black
18–19	04	Added: chimney
19–20	33–34	Added: ball
20	27	Added: sign
21–22	28	Added: lamp
22	23–24	Changed: pillar, yellow to green
22–24	26	Removed: awning
23–24	12–13	Removed: water tank
23–27	13–14	Added: roof
24–25	15–16	Changed: height of window
25–26	06–07	Changed: building, blue to red
25–26	19–20	Removed: wall segment
25–26	34–35	Removed: dog
26–28	11–12	Added: ladder
26–28	17	Added: roof unit
26–29	22–23	Changed: stained glass
26–29	33–34	Added: umbrella
28	03–04	Removed: building
28–29	11–12	Added: graffiti
28–29	14–15	Changed: roof unit, blue to yellow
28–29	35	Changed: shirt, red to blue
29	24–25	Added: decoration
30	04–06	Added: giant cigar

PUZZLE 24: Paris

PUZZLE 24: Paris

PUZZLE 24

Paris

The capital of France is situated on the River Seine. It is an important center of culture and fashion, and is famous for such architectural wonders as the Arc de Triomphe and the Eiffel Tower.

01	30	Added: flag
03–04	29	Removed: crossing
04–05	29–31	Changed: height of sculpture
05	29	Changed: vehicle, blue to red
06–07	13–14	Added: buildings
07–08	06–07	Removed: building
08	31–32	Changed: height of sculpture
09–10	07–09	Changed: building tilted
09–12	19	Added: sports field
09	20	Changed: height of pillar
10–11	17–18	Added: window
10	20–21	Added: building
10	32	Added: window
11–13	32	Changed: wall, orange to red
12–13	02	Added: giant olive
12–14	11	Added: girders
15	11–12	Added: windows
15–18	25–26	Changed: height of building
16	34–35	Changed: size of window
18–19	14–15	Removed: buildings
18	21	Removed: window
18–19	24	Removed: tower
18	35	Added: water tank
19	31	Changed: length of balcony
19–20	17–18	Changed: height of building
19–21	19–20	Changed: roof
19–20	33–34	Removed: ivy
20–21	29–30	Removed: roof unit
21–22	33–35	Added: windows
22–23	19–20	Changed: length of building
22–24	30–31	Added: bushes
22–23	32	Removed: wall
23	31	Added: window
23–24	32–33	Removed: windows
24	19–20	Changed: roof
24–26	26–27	Changed: roof, red to blue
25	20	Changed: roof unit, red to white
25	24	Changed: window, black to red
25	34–35	Changed: length of building
26	28–30	Removed: stripe
26–27	31–32	Removed: windows
26–27	34	Added: turret
27–28	25–26	Added: windows
27	30	Changed: roof unit
27	34–35	Changed: window
28	07–08	Added: building
28–29	10–12	Added: Arc de Triomphe
28	24–25	Removed: chimney
29–30	31–32	Changed: length of building
30	01–02	Added: glider

PUZZLE 25: San Sebastián

PUZZLE 25: San Sebastián

PUZZLE 25

San Sebastián

San Sebastián (also known as Donostia) is a Spanish coastal city located on the Bay of Biscay. It is an important cultural center and one of Spain's largest tourist attractions.

01	28	Removed: dog
02–05	04–05	Added: seagull
02	24–27	Removed: lamppost
03–05	16–17	Changed: building, orange to green
03–06	27–28	Changed: size of steps
04–08	11	Removed: hilltop
04–05	22–23	Removed: window
05–07	12	Removed: building
06–07	13	Removed: building
06–07	17–19	Changed: width of building
06–07	20–21	Removed: chimney
08–09	25–27	Added: tree
08–09	29–30	Added: seagull
10–12	13–14	Changed: length of building
10–13	15	Changed: roof, red to green
10–13	19	Changed: roof, red to green
10	22–23	Removed: window
10–11	25–28	Added: lamppost
12–13	20	Removed: window
13–14	30–31	Added: beach ball
13–15	33–35	Removed: pole
14–15	22	Removed: window
15–17	09–10	Changed: height of building
15–18	22	Changed: roof, red to green
17–18	17–19	Changed: building
17	25–28	Added: lamppost
18–19	20–21	Removed: chimney
19–20	27–28	Removed: figures
20	10–12	Changed: width of building
21–22	11	Removed: tower detail
21–23	14–16	Added: building section
21	25–28	Added: lamppost
22	11–12	Added: arch window
22	25	Removed: person
23–25	07	Added: cloud
23	22–23	Removed: window
24–25	09–10	Removed: tower
24–28	17	Changed: balcony, yellow to red
25–26	12–13	Added: archway
26–30	09–10	Removed: trees
26–28	17–18	Added: wall
26	35	Removed: people
27–30	14	Changed: roof, red to green
27	20–21	Removed: logo
27–28	22	Removed: window
27	27–28	Added: pillar
27–30	32–35	Added: tree
28	23	Added: graffiti
29–30	24–28	Added: tree
30	21	Removed: window

PUZZLE 26: Auckland

ANZ
TELCO

PUZZLE 26: Auckland

PUZZLE 26

Auckland

Auckland is New Zealand's largest urban area, located in the country's North Island. It is the warmest, sunniest, and most cosmopolitan of New Zealand's major cities.

01–03	07	Added: peninsula
01–03	15–16	Changed: building, orange to blue
01–02	28–30	Changed: wall
02–03	17–19	Added: windows
04–06	19–25	Added: row of trees
05–06	19–20	Changed: size of building
07–08	12	Changed: sign, blue to red
07–08	15	Removed: stripe
07	19–20	Removed: window
08–09	20–21	Added: pillars
8–11	11	Removed: boat
09	33–35	Removed: vehicle
10–11	27–30	Changed: wall, red to white
11–12	26–27	Removed: sloping roof
11–15	31–33	Changed: neon sign color, yellow to blue
12	12	Added: crane
12	14	Removed: letters
12–14	19–21	Changed: width of building
12	26–27	Changed: door open
13	29	Added: air conditioning unit
13	14–15	Changed: height of banner
14–15	13–14	Changed: length of roof unit
14–16	17–18	Added: red wall
14–15	25–26	Changed: height of roof unit
15–16	11–13	Changed: height of building
15–16	18–19	Added: soccer player
16–24	02–06	Added: volcanic eruption
17–19	13–14	Changed: height of roof
17–19	15–19	Changed: building, green to blue
17	30	Removed: window
19–20	10–11	Changed: length of pier
20	21–22	Removed: banner
20–21	26–27	Removed: stripe
21–23	13–15	Added: building
21–22	18–20	Added: billboard
21	28–30	Added: giant Santa
22–24	09–10	Removed: wharf
22	21–22	Added: roof unit
23–30	07–08	Added: wave
23–24	13–15	Changed: top of building
23–24	22–23	Changed: shape of roof
23–25	27–29	Removed: hole in building
24–27	09	Removed: top of building
25	20–21	Added: window divider
26	22	Removed: window
26–27	13–15	Removed: building
26–27	26–27	Changed: squares darker
26–29	32–34	Changed: color of roof, blue to red
27–28	14–17	Removed: pillar
27–28	27	Added: air conditioner

PUZZLE 27: Venice

PUZZLE 27

Venice

Venice is a city in northeastern Italy, situated on 118 small islands linked by bridges. Its famous waterways and its long tradition of art and architecture have made it a major tourist destination.

01–03	01–02	Changed: height of building
01–03	28–30	Removed: oar
01–02	33–34	Removed: boat detail
02–03	15–21	Added: pole
03–05	06–07	Changed: height of building
03–04	27–28	Changed: shirt, red to blue
06–07	06–10	Removed: scaffold
06–09	18–19	Removed: oars
06–08	20–21	Removed: oar
06–07	30–31	Removed: oar support
07–11	02–04	Changed: height of building
07	14–15	Removed: canoeist
07–13	24–25	Removed: oar
09–10	18–20	Changed: tunic, red to purple
11–12	06–11	Changed: wall, pink to blue
12–13	03–05	Removed: building
13–15	05–08	Changed: wall, brown to green
13–15	14–15	Changed: shirts, red to purple
14–15	21–23	Changed: shirt, red to blue
15–16	15–22	Added: oar
15–20	31–33	Removed: oar
16–17	03–04	Added: dormer
16–17	19–20	Changed: shirt, red to blue
16–17	24–25	Removed: "5"
17–18	33–35	Removed: oar support
19	13–27	Added: pole
20–21	30–32	Changed: tunic, blue to green
21–23	03–04	Added: window
21–22	12	Added: sign
21	14–15	Removed: yellow panel
21	18–19	Removed: canoeist
21	27–28	Removed: face
23	13–16	Removed: pole
24–26	11–12	Changed: umbrella, green to purple
24–27	16–17	Changed: cover, blue to green
24–25	26–27	Removed: oar
24–26	28–31	Changed: tunic, blue to green
25–26	03–06	Added: building section
26–27	07–08	Removed: windows
26–27	13–14	Added: sign
26–27	19–31	Added: oar
26	33–34	Removed: oar support
27–29	03–04	Removed: windows
28	01	Removed: chimney
28–30	28	Removed: oar
29	05–08	Removed: window
29	14–18	Added: pole
29–30	24–25	Removed: paddle
30	02–04	Removed: window
30	06–10	Changed: building, yellow to purple

PUZZLE 28: Lviv

WELCOME
Morshinska

PUZZLE 28: Lviv

PUZZLE 28

Lviv

One of Ukraine's major cultural cities, Lviv was founded in 1240 and has previously been the capital of the Galicia region, absorbed into the Kingdom of Poland, and part of the Soviet Union.

01	21–22	Added: chimney
01	25–26	Changed: window
01	31–32	Added: street lamp
02	29–30	Added: potted plant
03–04	10–11	Added: skylight
03–04	33–34	Removed: lamppost
04	05–06	Changed: wall, blue to yellow
04–08	26–28	Changed: shop façade
06–07	05–06	Added: tunnel
06	15–16	Added: ladder
08–09	05–06	Changed: roof
08–09	10	Added: dormer
08–09	16–17	Added: tree
10	05	Changed: tower, green to red
10	10	Removed: chimney
10–11	14–15	Changed: size of roof
10–11	18–19	Added: chimney
10–11	28–29	Changed: image reversed
11–14	07–09	Changed: buildings merged
11–14	24–25	Changed: ledge, blue to yellow
12	19–20	Changed: roof unit, white to brown
12–13	25	Added: decoration
13–15	17–18	Changed: roof gradient
13	26–27	Changed: direction of person
14–15	14–15	Changed: awning, grey to blue
14	24	Changed: size of window
14–15	30–31	Removed: manhole cover
15–16	01	Removed: building
15–17	05–06	Added: building
15–16	17–18	Removed: brickwork
16–17	09–10	Added: sign
17–18	07–08	Removed: balcony
17–18	09	Removed: vehicle
18–19	05–06	Removed: building
18–19	06–09	Changed: height of pillar
18–19	12–13	Added: skylight
19–20	33–34	Changed: direction of cart
21–24	07–08	Changed: roof, brown to grey
21–22	14–17	Added: buttress
22–23	01–02	Changed: height of building
23	14–16	Removed: window
23	32	Removed: person
24–25	05–06	Removed: tower
25–27	13–16	Changed: size of steeple
25–27	23–24	Changed: size of dormer
26–30	01–08	Changed: steeple, green to bronze
26	34–35	Changed: size of person
27–28	20–21	Changed: size of chimney
28	14–18	Added: window
28–29	16–17	Changed: vehicle, white to red

PUZZLE 29: Amsterdam

PUZZLE 29: Amsterdam

PUZZLE 29

Amsterdam

Amsterdam is the capital city of the Kingdom of the Netherlands. It has many world-renowned attractions including the Van Gough Museum and the Anne Frank House, as well as its historic canals and coffeeshops.

01–05	10–14	Changed: roof, red to green
01–03	14–20	Added: foliage
01	23–24	Removed: front wheel
01	25–27	Changed: panel, orange to blue
02–04	21–23	Changed: doors, blue to red
02–04	27	Changed: size of fender
03	16–17	Removed: window
03–06	25–26	Changed: boat, brown to blue
06–07	07–10	Added: foliage
06	21–23	Changed: length of container
06–08	26–28	Removed: chain
07–09	23–24	Removed: handlebar
09–10	14–15	Changed: wall, red to green
09–10	34–35	Removed: shadow
10–12	10–11	Added: seagull
10	16–17	Removed: window
10–11	22–23	Added: shadow
11–13	28–31	Changed: fender, pink to purple
12–14	23–24	Added: boat
12–14	25–26	Changed: direction of seat
12–13	29–30	Removed: spoke
14–15	32	Changed: length of stand
15–16	13–15	Changed: roof, red to green
16	21–23	Removed: bridge support
16–17	07–09	Removed: spire

17–18	12–13	Removed: dormer
18–20	18–11	Added: tower
18	14–15	Removed: window
18	19–20	Changed: height of window
19	12–13	Removed: chimney
19	17–18	Removed: window
19	20	Removed: sign
19	25–26	Removed: lamp
19–20	32–33	Changed: size of fender
20	11–13	Changed: chimney, red to green
20	13–15	Changed: roof, red to green
20	16–17	Removed: window
20–21	21–22	Added: seagull
21–24	07–08	Changed: height of dome base
21–22	18–19	Removed: lamppost
22–23	04–05	Removed: cross
22–23	09	Removed: window
22–23	26–29	Changed: balustrade
23–24	15–16	Removed: window
24	33–24	Removed: stand
24	12	Removed: window
25–30	01–09	Added: foliage
25	17–18	Removed: window
29–30	17–18	Removed: windows
29–30	19–25	Added: foliage

01
02
03
04
05
06
07
08
09
10
11
12
13
14
15
16
17
18
19
20
21
22
23
24
25
26
27
28
29
30
31
32
33
34
35

JUST DO IT.

PUZZLE 30: Los Angeles

PUZZLE 30

Los Angeles

The city of Los Angeles (also known simply as L.A.) is the most populous city of the west coast state of California, and the second most populated city in the United States.

01	17–19	Changed: height of building
01	35	Added: cylinder
02	28	Added: window panel
02–03	16	Added: window reflections
02–03	25–26	Added: building
03	32	Added: tree
03–04	19–20	Changed: size of recess
04	25	Added: windows
04	29	Changed: height of unit
04	34–35	Changed: length of storage
04–08	05	Added: superhero
05	23–24	Added: logo
05	33	Changed: windows
06–07	22	Added: stripes
06–07	30	Added: box unit
06	35	Added: street light
07	32	Changed: windows
08	16	Added: elevator
09	12–14	Added: reflection
09	26	Changed: balconies, red to blue
09	28	Removed: windows
09	33	Added: windows
09	35	Added: brown line
10	34	Added: rooftop unit
10–11	10–11	Removed: top of building
11	21–22	Removed: shadow
11	27–28	Changed: height of building
12	15	Changed: size of building
12	33	Added: column
13	35	Removed: window
13–18	07–10	Added: flying book
15	32	Removed: window
16	34	Added: gap
18	30	Removed: plants
18	31	Added: window
19	13	Removed: window
19	15	Changed: height of shadow
19	21–22	Added: dinosaur
19	35	Added: truck
20–21	34–35	Added: crane
21–23	07–09	Added: dragon
22	31	Changed: wall
23–24	33	Added: vehicle
24	18	Added: windows
24	35	Changed: vehicle, white to blue
24–25	24–25	Removed: window
27–29	31	Added: dinosaur
28–29	12	Changed: height of windows
29	26	Removed: windows
29	33	Removed: fence

PUZZLE 31: Vienna

PUZZLE 31

Vienna

Vienna is Austria's capital and its largest city. It has a rich history, particularly in the field of music. In the twenty-first century it has been lauded for its quality of life and innovation.

01–02	18–20	Changed: size of roof
01	33–34	Removed: people
01–02	34	Added: roof
02–03	32–33	Removed: balloon seller
03–05	26–27	Added: reflective windows
03–04	33	Removed: people
04–06	08–10	Removed: building
04–05	16–18	Changed: width of building
05–06	23–25	Added: windows
06–08	15	Changed: roof, red to green
06–09	33–35	Changed: roof, red to green
07	20–23	Removed: windows
07	32	Removed: person
08–09	17–19	Changed: roof, red to green
10	11	Removed: building
10–11	17–19	Changed: wall, orange to green
10	24–25	Added: window
10	26–27	Added: window
11	24–25	Removed: window
12	15	Changed: corner, red to green
13–14	18–21	Changed: size of roof annex
13	26	Removed: window
13–14	29–30	Added: cover
13	33	Removed: people
14–18	10–12	Changed: dome, green to red
15–16	33	Removed: people
16–17	08	Removed: building
16	13	Removed: window
16–18	14	Changed: roof, red to green
16	20	Removed: roof structure
16	23–24	Added: blind
16	29	Removed: window
16	34–35	Removed: people
17	26	Added: window blind
18–19	13	Changed: roof, green to red
19–20	08–10	Removed: crane
20–21	13–14	Changed: size of building
20	27	Removed: window
20–21	28–29	Removed: spires
21	19	Added: window
21	25	Removed: window
22–24	07–08	Added: building
23	24	Removed: window
23–26	28–31	Added: tiles
23–24	34–35	Removed: ornament
24–27	09	Removed: building
25	27–28	Removed: window
26–29	17–18	Removed: spire decoration
27–28	22–23	Removed: window
30	21–23	Added: stripe

PUZZLE 32: Tripoli

PUZZLE 32: Tripoli

PUZZLE 32

Tripoli

Tripoli is Libya's capital city. It was founded by the Phoenicians in the seventh century BC. Since then it has been occupied by—among others—Romans, Greeks, Normans, Arabs, Spanish, Ottomans, Italians, and British.

01–02	31–33	Changed: size of window
02–03	05–06	Removed: window
02	22–23	Added: window
04	06–07	Added: window
04–05	17–18	Added: water container
04–07	23–24	Changed: roof, green to pink
05	03–04	Removed: door
05–06	05–06	Removed: window
05–06	22–23	Removed: window
05–06	26–27	Removed: spire
05–07	29–31	Added: pigeon
05–06	33–35	Removed: window
07–10	01–03	Added: pigeon
07–08	17–18	Removed: door
08–09	05–06	Removed: window
09–11	04–05	Removed: window
09–10	24–26	Added: water container
09–11	30–32	Added: window
10	14–15	Removed: window
12–13	02	Removed: window
12–13	12–15	Changed: roof, red to green
13–17	33–35	Added: tree
14	05–06	Added: window
15	05–06	Removed: window
15–16	25–26	Removed: air conditioner
16	10–11	Removed: part of dome
16–17	19–20	Added: water container
16–17	29–30	Removed: window
18–19	03–04	Changed: spire, red to green
18–19	05–06	Removed: window
18–21	06–07	Changed: roof, red to green
18–19	17–18	Removed: window
19–20	27–28	Changed: size of window
21–23	19–20	Removed: arch
21	27–29	Changed: curtain, blue to red
21–33	31–32	Removed: window
22–24	21–22	Removed: water container
22–23	34–35	Removed: window
23–24	01–05	Removed: windows
23	08	Removed: window
23–24	11–12	Changed: size of wall
23–24	16	Added: window
25–26	05–06	Added: roof annex
25–27	34–35	Added: panel
26–27	11–12	Added: windows
26–27	13–14	Removed: window
26	22–24	Removed: window
26–28	26–28	Changed: stripes, red to green
27–29	08–09	Changed: roof, red to green
27	17	Removed: window

良縁祈
恋占いおみくじ
恋のお守り
参拝時間

良縁祈

PUZZLE 33: Kyoto

PUZZLE 33

Kyoto

Kyoto is the former imperial capital of Japan, located on the island of Honshu. The city is home to many of Japan's Nation Treasures, and is famous for its many shrines.

01–02	03	Added: corner
01–03	11–15	Changed: foliage, red to green
01–03	19–22	Added: topiary
01–03	33–35	Added: stone
03–07	30–31	Removed: crack
04–09	33–35	Added: bush
05–10	20–25	Added: bush
06–08	02–03	Added: bird
07–12	03–05	Changed: height of roof
07	09–10	Changed: motif, red to green
07–14	14–18	Added: bush
08	09–14	Added: column
08–10	31–33	Changed: height of signpost
10–15	25–28	Added: bush
10–13	34–35	Added: stone
13–15	05–06	Removed: stone section
13–14	32–34	Removed: arm
14	09–10	Changed: length of beam
15–16	12–13	Removed: writing
15	29	Added: flower
16–20	02–03	Added: roof detail
16–18	15	Changed: panel, orange to blue
17	10–12	Added: tassel
17	27	Removed: part of character
18–19	16–17	Added: engraving
18	20–21	Removed: protrusion
18–22	33–35	Changed: shirt, pink to blue
19–20	10–12	Added: tassel
20–21	12	Added: decoration
20–21	22–23	Added: steps
21	10–11	Removed: decoration
22	30–31	Changed: scarf, purple to green
22–23	14–15	Added: lantern
22–25	01–03	Added: foliage
23–25	33–35	Changed: bag, red to green
24	10–12	Added: tassel
24–25	14	Added: light
24	20–21	Changed: flower, pink to blue
25–26	09–11	Added: decoration
25–26	14–15	Added: dark panel
25	19	Added: writing
25–26	21	Added: flower
25–26	24	Changed: fabric, red to blue
26–27	09–11	Added: tassel
26–27	17–19	Added: pillar
26	19–20	Changed: hat, red to green
27–28	25–30	Changed: bag, yellow to red
27–30	31–35	Added: bush
29	18–19	Removed: writing
29–30	14–15	Added: lantern

PUZZLE 34: Seattle

PUZZLE 34

Seattle

Seattle is a coastal seaport city in the state of Washington, and is the largest city in the Pacific Northwest region of the United States. A noteworthy feature of its cityscape is the Space Needle, the iconic observation tower built in 1962.

01–08	02–04	Added: cloud
01–05	08	Changed: height of mountain
01	10–11	Changed: height of building
01	12–14	Changed: height of building
01	17–19	Changed: building, white to green
02	10–11	Changed: height of building
02	17–19	Changed: width of building
02–04	34–35	Changed: size of building
03–06	19–20	Added: trees
04–05	10–11	Removed: buildings
04–06	17–18	Changed: building
04	28	Added: window
04	30	Added: tree
05	12–13	Removed: building
05	13	Changed: dome, blue to red
05–06	18	Changed: size of building
05–06	20–21	Removed: building section
06–08	13–15	Changed: height of building
06	29	Added: vehicle
08–09	12–13	Removed: building
09	15	Changed: width of building
09–10	17	Changed: size of building
09	20–22	Removed: windows
09–14	28–30	Changed: size of building
11–16	11	Removed: buildings

11–12	19–22	Added: tower block
12–13	08–09	Added: airplane
12–13	15–17	Changed: building, red to green
13–14	17–19	Added: building
13–14	26–27	Removed: tree
16–17	22–23	Removed: building
17–19	16–18	Changed: height of building
17–19	24–27	Changed: width of building
18	10	Removed: tower
19	21–22	Changed: wall, orange to green
20–22	23	Removed: building
20	24–25	Added: antenna
20	25	Added: window
21	16–17	Removed: pole
22–24	16–17	Changed: height of building
22	25–26	Added: window
24–26	12–13	Changed: size of island
24–25	15	Removed: boat
25	26	Removed: vehicles
25–28	33–34	Changed: length of building
27–29	06–07	Added: seagull
27–28	25	Added: platform
28–29	12–13	Added: storage tanks
29	16–18	Removed: support
30	13–14	Removed: boat

PUZZLE 35: Milan

PUZZLE 35

Milan

The sprawling metropolis of Milan is Italy's largest city and its commercial heart. It is a world-renowned center of art, design, and culture, and the home of two internationally successful soccer clubs.

01	07–08	Removed: spire
01–02	30	Removed: shadow
01–02	32	Removed: shadow
01	33–34	Removed: people
02–03	21	Removed: person and shadow
02	25–26	Removed: person
05–06	19–20	Removed: car and people
05–07	23–24	Removed: person and shadow
05–06	24	Removed: shadow
05–06	30–32	Added: plants and flag
07–08	21–22	Removed: police vehicle
07–09	32–35	Changed: handrail, red to green
08	08	Removed: building
09–10	09–10	Changed: size of wall
10	07–08	Added: building
10–12	33	Removed: shadow
11–12	23–24	Changed: size of stall
11–14	31–32	Removed: person and shadow
11–14	34	Removed: shadow
12	11–12	Removed: window
12	16–17	Removed: column
13	19–21	Changed: sign, blue to red
13	25	Removed: person
14–16	22–24	Changed: height of stall
14	35	Removed: person

15–16	10–16	Added: column
17–22	09–10	Removed: plaque
18–20	16	Added: archway base
19–20	26	Removed: person
19	28–29	Removed: person
19–20	32–33	Removed: shadow
20	11–12	Removed: arch decoration
20	20–21	Removed: shadow
20–22	34	Removed: shadow
21–24	03–05	Removed: skylight
23	18	Removed: balcony detail
23	31–32	Removed: person
24	34–35	Removed: person
25–29	33–35	Added: awning
26	14–18	Added: column
26	23–29	Added: shadow
26	30–31	Removed: trash can
28–30	21–22	Added: stone decoration
29	15–18	Removed: column
29	12	Added: stonework
29–30	23–24	Removed: umbrella
29–30	26–27	Removed: part of shadow
29–30	29	Removed: writing
29–30	31–32	Changed: awning
30	06	Removed: stonework

PUZZLE 36: Ho Chi Minh City

PUZZLE 36

Ho Chi Minh City

The largest city in Vietnam, Ho Chi Minh City was previously known as Saigon (under French colonial rule) until it was captured by the People's Army of Vietnam and Viet Cong in 1975. Today it is the economic center of the country.

01–02	03–05	Changed: height of building
01–03	22–26	Changed: wall, blue to purple
01–02	28	Changed: length of roof
02–03	33–35	Changed: wall, brown to green
03–04	20	Removed: chimney
03–05	33–35	Changed: width of roof
04–06	01–03	Removed: building
04–06	09–10	Changed: building, green to purple
05–06	26–17	Changed: roof, brown to green
07–09	21–22	Added: roof section
08–09	12–14	Changed: building, yellow to blue
08–09	16	Changed: roof, red to green
08–09	18	Removed: window
08–09	24	Removed: window
09–10	19	Removed: window
09–10	26	Removed: window
09–10	28–29	Changed: length of wall
10–11	02–03	Changed: height of building
10–12	09–10	Changed: building, yellow to blue
10–13	31–32	Changed: width of roof
11–19	10–11	Changed: roof, red to green
11	19–20	Removed: window
13–15	05–07	Changed: height of building
13	22–23	Removed: window
14–15	25	Removed: window

15	20–21	Removed: window
15–17	35	Added: roof section
16–18	31	Changed: awning, green to red
17–18	05–06	Changed: height of building
17	17	Removed: window
17–20	21	Changed: wall, red to green
18–20	15–16	Changed: building, yellow to red
19–20	01–02	Removed: building
19–24	10–11	Changed: roof, brown to green
19–20	34–35	Added: door
20	07–08	Changed: height of building
21–22	23	Changed: size of roof
22–23	01–02	Changed: height of building
22–23	07–08	Changed: building, red to green
24–26	21	Changed: roof, red to green
25	01–03	Removed: building
25–26	12	Removed: window
26–27	14–15	Removed: window
26–28	20	Changed: width of roof
26–28	22–23	Changed: roof, red to green
27–28	09–10	Changed: building, pink to green
28–30	18–19	Changed: height of building
28–30	25	Removed: window
28–29	27–28	Changed: wall, gray to red
29–30	34–35	Changed: size of roof

PUZZLE 37: Sarajevo

PUZZLE 37: Sarajevo

PUZZLE 37

Sarajevo

Sarajevo is the capital and largest city of Bosnia and Herzegovina. It is famous for its religious and cultural diversity, and features an impressive collection of cathedrals, mosques, and synagogues.

04	19	Removed: hole in bridge
04–05	16–17	Removed: vehicle
04–05	33–34	Changed: sign reversed
05	30–31	Removed: person
06–08	07–08	Changed: height of building
06–07	24–26	Changed: position of bus
06	30	Changed: direction of arrow
07–08	22	Added: vehicle
08–10	08–09	Added: building
08	32–33	Changed: sign to monument
09–10	25	Removed: panel
09–10	35	Removed: streetlight
10–11	33–34	Changed: vehicle, red to green
11	30–31	Changed: window to balcony
14–15	04	Removed: tower
14	27–28	Changed: decoration reversed
14	34	Changed: sign, yellow to blue
15–16	10	Changed: dome, green to orange
15	14–15	Changed: annex, pink to green
15	15–16	Added: window
16–17	13–21	Added: tower
16	31–35	Added: pole
17–18	09–10	Changed: slope of roof
18	11	Added: dome
18	12	Added: window
18–19	31	Removed: window
19–20	04–05	Added: building
20–24	04–05	Changed: direction of crane
20–21	09–10	Changed: wall, yellow to blue
20	26	Removed: panel
20	27–28	Changed: blinds
21	08–09	Added: spire
21	17–18	Added: window
21–22	10	Added: windows
21–22	24–25	Changed: chimney
22–23	06–07	Changed: window pattern
22–23	30–31	Changed: length of windows
23–25	18–19	Changed: building, yellow to blue
24	28	Removed: satellite dish
25–30	01–02	Added: hill
26	05–08	Changed: width of building
26	11–12	Changed: height of tower
26	22	Removed: window
26–27	10	Added: chimney
26–28	33–34	Changed: roof, green to brown
28–29	06	Changed: oval, purple to orange
28–29	12	Removed: dormer
28–30	21	Changed: roof, red to purple
28–29	24–25	Removed: dormer window
29	07	Added: building section

PUZZLE 38: San Francisco

PUZZLE 38

San Francisco

San Francisco is a consolidated city-county and an important cultural and financial center of California. Its many attractions include the Golden Gate Bridge, Fisherman's Wharf, Alcatraz Island, and the oldest Chinatown in the United States.

01	30–35	Added: pole
01–02	08–09	Changed: length of building
02	23–24	Changed: height of wall
02	26	Removed: window
02–03	28–29	Added: pipes
03–04	12	Removed: roof section
06–08	16–19	Added: tree
06–08	32	Removed: cars
07–08	04	Removed: light on treetop
07–08	08	Removed: light on treetop
07–08	28–29	Removed: truck
08–10	14–15	Added: seagull
09–10	27–28	Removed: dog, walker, road marking "STOP"
09–10	35	Removed: road marking "STOP"
11–16	34–35	Added: treetop
11–12	26–27	Removed: red and blue signs
12–13	14–15	Added: enlarged treetop
13–15	22–23	Changed: size of roof section
15–16	07	Removed: window
15	08	Removed: blue door
15	14	Removed: window
15–16	16–17	Removed: window
17	06	Added: window
17–18	31	Added: pipes
17–18	35	Changed: edge of rooftop
18–19	01	Removed: tree
18–21	09–10	Removed: rooftop
18–19	20–21	Changed: extended rooftop
18	28	Added: window
18–19	35	Removed: chimney
19–21	05	Changed: height of building
19–20	11	Removed: window
19	14	Removed: window
19–21	33–34	Changed: roof fence, green to pink
20–21	13	Removed: window
20–21	18–19	Changed: doorway to window bay
20–21	26–27	Removed: sign
21–23	28–29	Removed: sign
21–22	34–35	Added: roof wall
22–23	04–05	Removed: window
22	10	Removed: window
22–23	18	Removed: windows
24–26	12–13	Added: extra story to building
25–27	34–35	Added: top of window bay
26–30	28	Changed: length of rooftop
26–27	29–30	Changed: gap between window bay
27–28	06–07	Removed: window
29–30	05	Added: extra story to building
28–30	11–12	Added: extra story to building
28	17	Removed: window

PUZZLE 39: Shanghai

PUZZLE 39: Shanghai

PUZZLE 39

Shanghai

Shanghai is the most populous city in the world. Located on the Yangtze River Delta in the People's Republic of China, it is also the world's busiest container port.

01	09	Removed: building section
01–02	30	Removed: road marking
01–02	34	Changed: vehicle, orange to green
02	09–10	Changed: height of building
02–03	14–15	Changed: height of building
02	23–24	Removed: support column
03–04	03–05	Changed: height of building
03	07–08	Changed: height of building section
03–05	11–12	Changed: height of building
03–04	21	Removed: vehicle
04–05	10	Removed: building section
04–06	26	Removed: vehicle
05–06	31–32	Changed: vehicle, red to blue
05	24–25	Removed: support column
05–09	16–17	Changed: roof, red to green
06–07	24–25	Added: support column
07–08	08–09	Removed: building
07–09	14–15	Changed: length of building
07	21	Added: support column
08	32–33	Removed: road marking
09–10	24	Removed: vehicle
09	29	Removed: road marking
10–11	33–34	Removed: road marking
11–12	10–11	Changed: height of building
13–15	09–10	Changed: height of building
13–15	25	Removed: road marking
15–16	27–28	Removed: vehicle
15–16	10–11	Removed: building
16–17	07–08	Changed: height of building
17–18	17–19	Changed: length of building
18	20–21	Removed: support column
18–19	24–25	Removed: vehicle
18–19	31	Removed: road marking
18	33	Changed: sign, blue to pink
19	05–06	Removed: building section
22–23	24	Removed: sign
23	09	Removed: building section
23–25	15–16	Removed: building section
23	21	Added: road sign
23–24	33–34	Removed: road marking
24–25	07–08	Changed: height of building
24–25	28–29	Removed: road marking
26–27	10–11	Removed: building
26	23–25	Removed: support column
26–27	30–33	Added: support column
27–28	08–09	Changed: height of building
28–29	12–13	Changed: height of building
30	07–10	Removed: building
30	28	Removed: vehicle
30	32–33	Removed: support column

PUZZLE 40: Lima

01 02 03 04 05 06 07 08 09 10 11 12 13 14 15 16 17 18 19 20 21 22 23 24 25 26 27 28 29 30
01 02 03 04 05 06 07 08 09 10 11 12 13 14 15 16 17 18 19 20 21 22 23 24 25 26 27 28 29 30 31 32 33 34 35

PUZZLE 40

Lima

Lima is the capital of Peru, located in the valleys of three rivers. It is home to one of the oldest universities in the world—the National University of San Marcos, which was established in 1551.

01–03	17–20	Changed: building, brown to green
03–06	13–14	Added: blue paint
03–04	18–19	Added: fence
03–04	24–25	Removed: window
03–04	27–28	Added: tree
05–08	01–03	Removed: building
05–06	10–11	Added: window
05	24	Added: spigot
05–06	34–35	Added: water tank
08–13	19–21	Changed: floors swapped
09–13	30–31	Changed: building, green to red
09–12	33–35	Removed: street light
11	04–05	Removed: door
11–12	26–27	Removed: red bricks
12	02	Changed: window, green to red
13	22–23	Added: person
14–16	22–23	Added: foliage
14–17	27–28	Removed: foundation
15	15–16	Added: water tank
15–18	20–21	Changed: building, purple to brown
16–17	26–27	Added: window
17–18	18–19	Changed: size of arch
17–19	25–26	Added: shack
17	31–32	Removed: window
18–20	05–06	Changed: base of building, red to grey
18–20	16–17	Changed: wall, orange to red
18–21	19	Removed: brickwork
18–20	26–27	Removed: building
19–20	23–25	Removed: pole and wires
19–21	29–32	Added: walkway
20–21	10	Changed: wall, white to yellow
20	22	Added: window
21–23	20–21	Added: clothesline
22–23	08–09	Changed: darkened window
22–23	12–13	Added: steps
22–24	15–17	Added: green wall
22–26	31	Changed: base of building, red to brown
23	34–35	Removed: pillar
24–28	03–05	Removed: room on roof
24–25	13	Removed: window
24–26	22	Changed: wall
24–25	25–26	Changed: size of window
25–26	08–09	Changed: wall, orange to blue
26–27	28–29	Removed: window
27–28	30–31	Changed: width of wall
28–30	05–06	Added: graffiti
28–29	11–12	Added: water tank
29	02–03	Changed: wall, red to blue
30	29–30	Removed: window
30	34	Added: window

Credits

The publishers would like to thank the following sources for their kind permission to reproduce the photos in this book.

page 16 Getty Images/Photolibrary, page 20 Shutterstock/Mikadun, page 24 Shutterstock/fototehnik, page 28 Shutterstock/Sean Pavone, page 32 Shutterstock/Baloncici, page 36 Shutterstock/r.nagy, page 40 Shutterstock/Luciano Mortula, page 44 Shutterstock/Radiokafka, page 48 Shutterstock/Songquan Deng, page 52 Shutterstock/michaeljung, page 56 Shutterstock/Neale Cousland, page 60 Shutterstock/Boris Stroujko, page 64 Shutterstock/danm12, page 68 Shutterstock/Ivan Cheung, page 72 Shutterstock/leoks, page 76 Shutterstock/Luiz Rocha, page 80 Shutterstock/Np, page 84 Shutterstock/Sean Pavone, page 88 Shutterstock/Mikadun, page 92 Shutterstock/Patricia Hofmeester, page 96 Shutterstock/Andrey Bayda, page 100 Shutterstock/Sebastien Burel, page 104 Getty Images/Kevin Leighton, page 108 Shutterstock/Tupungato, page 112 Shutterstock/sunsinger, page 116 Getty Images/Chris Gin, page 120 Getty Images/Axel Fassio, page 124 Shutterstock/De Visu, page 128 Shutterstock/Leoks, page 132 Shutterstock/Sean Pavone, page 136 Shutterstock/Sergey Novikov, page 140 Getty Images/Lonely Planet Images, page 144 Shutterstock/Pigprox, page 148 Getty Images/Space Images, page 152 Shutterstock/Karol Kozlowski, page 156 Shutterstock/Kieukieuanh, page 160 Shutterstock/Mesut Dogan, page 164 Getty Images/Sigfrid López, page 168 Getty Images/Lonely Planet Images, page 172 Getty Images/David Milne/Moment

Every effort has been made to acknowledge correctly and contact the source and/or copyright holder of each picture. Carlton Books Limited apologizes for any unintentional errors or omissions, which will be corrected in future editions of this book.

Publishing Credits

Editorial Manager: Roland Hall
Editorial: Malcolm Croft
Puzzle checking: Richard Cater, Caroline Curtis, Richard Wolfrik Galland

Puzzle Creators: Danny Baldwin, Ryan Forshaw, Georgios Mardas

Designer: Tasha Lockyer
Creative Director: Clare Baggaley

Picture Research: Steve Behan

For Baker & Taylor:
Traci Douglas and Lori Asbury